BUILDING BASIC
English Skills

AGS Publishing
Circle Pines, Minnesota 55014-1796
800-328-2560

AGS Publishing is a trademark of American Guidance Service, Inc.

Printed in the United States of America

Product Number 93681
ISBN 0-7854-3358-9
A 0 9 8 7 6 5 4 5 3 2 1

CONTENTS

LESSON 1   What Is a Sentence?

KEY WORDS

Sentence
a group of words that expresses a complete thought

Sentence fragment
a group of words that does not express a complete thought

A **sentence** is a group of words that expresses a complete thought. Every sentence begins with a capital letter. Every sentence ends with a punctuation mark. Some groups of words have a capital letter and a punctuation mark. But they do not express a complete thought. These groups of words are not sentences. They are **sentence fragments**.

Example   Went shopping at the mall.

Step 1: Does the group of words begin with a capital letter and end with a period?

Went ← Yes. The first word begins with a capital letter.

mall. ← Yes. There is a period after *mall*.

Step 2: Do the words express a complete thought?

Went shopping at the mall.
No. The words do not express a complete thought. They do not name the person or people who went to the mall. The group of words is a sentence fragment.

Step 3: Write *S* on the line if the group of words is a sentence. Write *SF* on the line if the group of words is a sentence fragment.

Went shopping at the mall.   **SF**

A Read each group of words. Write *S* on the line if the group of words is a sentence. Write *SF* on the line if it is a sentence fragment.

1. Ron washed his car today. _____

2. Just before the play. _____

3. Due to the snowstorm. _____

4. Tess passed the salt. _____

5. Ann studied for the test. _____

6. While his girlfriend. _____

7. Sophie played alone. _____

8. Did you meet Tim? _____

9. Rose made lunch for us. _____

10. Ran quickly down the block. _____

A sentence fragment has a missing a part. You can add the missing part to change the fragment into a sentence.

Example Spoke to the students.

Step 1: Decide what is missing.

Spoke to the students. ◄— The sentence fragment does not name *who* spoke to the students.

Step 2: Identify words you might add to complete the sentence. Make a list of people who might speak to students.

teacher, principal, guest speaker

Step 3: Add words to complete the sentence.

The teacher spoke to the students.
The principal spoke to the students.
The guest speaker spoke to the students.

B Add words to make each sentence fragment a complete sentence.

1. The frightened puppy _____.

2. _____are going to the movies tonight.

3. _____cheered for the football team.

4. A brightly colored butterfly _____.

5. Before work, Ryan _____.

6. _____danced across the stage.

7. _____woke the sleeping baby.

8. _____carried their tents into the woods.

9. A swarm of angry bees _____.

10. After the baseball game, Chris _____.

LESSON 2   Subjects and Predicates

KEY WORDS

Subject
the part of a sentence that tells who or what the sentence is about

Predicate
the part of a sentence that tells something about the subject; it always contains a verb

Verb
a word that shows action or a state of being

Every sentence has two main parts. One part is the **subject**. The subject tells who or what the sentence is about. The other part is the **predicate**. The predicate tells something about the subject. Every predicate contains a **verb**. A verb is a word that shows action or a state of being.

Example My math teacher lives next door to me.

Step 1: Look for the words that tell who or what the sentence is about. Underline the subject.

<u>**My math teacher**</u> lives next door to me.

Step 2: Find the words that tell something about the subject, the math teacher. Circle the predicate.

Lives next door to me tells about the subject.

<u>My math teacher</u> (lives next door to me.)

 Read each sentence. Underline the subject. Circle the predicate.

1. My brother plays baseball every day.

2. The excited puppy ran to the group of teenagers.

3. The school basketball team won the state championship.

4. Dan and Juan went to the concert.

5. A colorful rainbow crossed the sky.

6. My next-door neighbor teaches at Oak High School.

7. Hundreds of cheering fans clapped for the band.

8. Ted's old car is broken again.

9. Mayor Jones spoke to our class.

10. Rita and her sister work at the hospital.

B More practice. These sentence fragments contain subjects. Add a predicate to make each sentence fragment a complete sentence.

1. A silly clown _____ .

2. Members of the school band _____ .

3. A stray cat _____ .

4. My noisy alarm clock _____ .

5. The Diaz family _____ .

C More practice. These sentence fragments contain predicates. Add a subject to make each sentence fragment a complete sentence.

1. _____ hid under the bed.

2. _____ tasted delicious.

3. _____ woke the sleeping baby.

4. _____ visited their old school.

5. _____ swam in the ocean.

LESSON 3 | # Beginning and Ending a Sentence

KEY WORDS

Capital letter
the uppercase form of
a letter, such as A, B, C

End punctuation
a period (.), question
mark (?), or exclamation
point (!) that shows
where a sentence ends

All sentences are alike in two ways. The first word of every sentence starts with a **capital letter**. The last word of every sentence is followed by an **end punctuation** mark. An end punctuation mark can be a period, a question mark, or an exclamation point. Use periods for sentences that are commands or facts. Use question marks for sentences that ask questions. Use exclamation points for sentences that express strong feelings.

Example | did you see Will's new car it is a shiny red sports car
i hope he gives me a ride in it soon

Step 1: Find the first group of words that expresses a complete thought.

did you see Will's new car is a complete thought.

Step 2: Capitalize the first word of the sentence. Put an end punctuation mark after the last word of the sentence.

Did you see Will's new car**?**

Step 3: Find the next group of words that expresses a complete thought.

it is a shiny red sports car is a complete thought.

Step 4: Capitalize the first word of the sentence. Put an end punctuation mark after the last word of the sentence.

Did you see Will's new car? **I**t is a shiny red sports car**.**

Step 5: Find the last group of words that expresses a complete thought.

i hope he gives me a ride in it soon is a complete thought.

Step 6: Capitalize the first word of the sentence. Put an end punctuation mark after the last word of the sentence.

Did you see Will's new car? It is a shiny red sports car. **I** hope he gives me a ride in it soon**!**

A Find the four sentences in each paragraph. List them on the lines. Capitalize the first word. End each sentence with the correct punctuation.

1. a terrible storm struck our town last night high winds knocked down power lines many homes lost electricity it will take days for things to get back to normal

_____

_____

_____

_____

2. is there a computer in your household millions of homes are equipped with this tool computers have become as common as television sets can you imagine living without this popular tool

_____

_____

_____

_____

3. tonight is Kim's surprise party her friends have been making plans for weeks more than thirty people will attend everyone will have a great time

_____

_____

_____

_____

B More practice. Write four sentences about your favorite childhood toy. Begin each sentence with a capital letter. End each sentence with the correct punctuation.

_____

_____

_____

_____

LESSON 4   Using Commas

KEY WORDS

Comma
a punctuation mark (,) used to separate words or groups of words

A **comma** is a punctuation mark used to separate words. Sometimes commas separate groups of words. Commas often are used in written dates and addresses. Dates and addresses have more than one part. Put a comma after each part to separate them.

Example   Julie was born on October 29 1985. Her address is 5 Main Street Spring Lake New Jersey 11111.

Step 1: Look at the date Julie was born. Identify the two main parts of the date.

     October 29   **1985**

     Date   Year

Step 2: Place a comma between the date and the year.

Julie was born on October 29, 1985.

Step 3: Look at the address. Identify the parts of the address.

     5 Main Street   **Spring Lake**   **New Jersey 11111**

     Street   Town   State and Zip Code

Step 4: Place a comma between the street, town, and state.

Her address is 5 Main Street, Spring Lake, New Jersey 11111.

 Put commas in the dates and addresses in these sentences.

1. The prom will be held on May 5 2002.

2. My family moved to 555 Oak Street Lincoln Nebraska.

3. Ted works in San Antonio Texas.

4. Her new address is 210 Pine Street Apartment 3B Orlando Florida.

5. Sue is driving to Belleville Illinois.

6. The Garden Club will meet on February 14 2003.

7. The high school band is performing in Orlando Florida.

8. The first Shoe Shop Store opened on January 5 1998.

9. My sister lives in Omaha Nebraska.

10. We were married on May 7 1994.

Some sentences have extra words. These words are not needed to form a complete thought. Sometimes these words start the sentence. Sometimes these words are the name of a person. A comma sets off words that are not needed to form a complete thought.

Example No I do not want to see a movie. I told you that already Paul.

Step 1: Identify a word in the first sentence that could be left out.

No I do not want to see a movie. ←
└─ This part of the sentence could be left out.
    This part of the sentence forms a complete thought.

Step 2: Place a comma after the extra word.

No, I do not want to see a movie.

Step 3: Identify a word in the next sentence that could be left out.

I told you that already **Paul**. ←
└─ This part of the sentence forms a complete thought.
    This part of the sentence could be left out.

Step 4: Place a comma before the extra word.

I told you that already, Paul.

B **Put commas where needed in each sentence. Some sentences may have more than one comma.**

1. Mary the phone is for you.

2. Yes I passed the driving test.

3. Well what do you want to do Peter?

4. Now where did I leave my keys?

5. Joan already left the party Tim.

6. Yes I gave that sweater to Rose.

7. Did you eat lunch Paolo?

8. No I do not have any extra money Bob

9. Mrs. Ruiz your taxi is here.

10. Actually I think you are correct Sam.

LESSON 5   # Commas in a Series

KEY WORDS

Comma
a punctuation mark (,) used to separate words or groups of words

Series
a group of three or more similar words or groups of words

Some sentences have two words that do the same job. A **comma** separates these similar words.

Example   Liang wore her faded baggy jeans.

Step 1: Identify two words in the sentence that are similar.

Liang wore her **faded baggy** jeans.

Both words describe *jeans*.

Step 2: Place a comma between the two words.

Liang wore her faded, baggy jeans.

A **Place a comma between each pair of similar words.**

1. The tired thirsty children ran to the water fountain.

2. A tall thin stranger knocked on my front door.

3. Our town was hit by a powerful dangerous storm.

4. Nell is a serious alert driver.

5. Kate took the soggy wrinkled clothes out of the washer.

6. A small plump bird rested on my car.

7. Liz wore a long flowing gown to the prom.

8. A sharp silver object is stuck in the tire.

9. Flashes of bright jagged lightning crossed the sky.

10. Heat turned the lumpy wet batter into a moist delicious cake.

Some sentences have three or more words, or groups of words, that do the same job. These words are called words in a **series**. A comma separates words in a series. The word *and* comes before the last word in a series. A comma comes before the word *and*.

Example Pete Eric and Ryan play on the same baseball team.
Pete catches Eric hits and Ryan pitches.

Step 1: Identify words that do the same thing in the first sentence.

Pete Eric and **Ryan** play on the same baseball team.

Names of three players

Step 2: Place a comma between the first two names and before the *and*.

Pete, Eric, and Ryan play on the same baseball team.

Step 3: Identify similar groups of words in the second sentence.

Pete catches Eric hits and **Ryan pitches**.

Player's name and what he does

Step 4: Place a comma between the first two groups of words and before the *and*.

Pete catches, Eric hits, and Ryan pitches.

B Put commas where needed in each sentence.

1. Josie ordered a hot dog fries soup and a drink.

2. Did you work with Seth Rob and Keenu?

3. Mrs. Gold bought apples oranges pears and bananas at the market.

4. We drove through Virginia North Carolina South Carolina and Georgia on our way to Florida.

5. Tia made dinner set the table and washed the dishes.

6. Bicycling swimming and photography are my favorite hobbies.

7. Dan has served as treasurer vice president and president of the Student Council.

8. Conferences are held in the gym the library and the main office.

9. Rhea looked for the puppy under the bed in the closet and behind the chair.

10. My mother sister and grandmother waited for me at the train station.

LESSON 6   **Using Quotation Marks**

KEY WORDS

Quotation marks
the marks (" ") placed
at the beginning and
end of the words a
person said

Comma
a punctuation mark (,)
used to separate words
or groups of words

A sentence may state something that a person has said. **Quotation marks** are placed at the beginning of the speaker's exact words. They are also placed at the end of the speaker's exact words. A **comma** is placed between the speaker's name and his or her words. The end punctuation goes inside the quotation marks. Use a question mark for the end punctuation if the speaker asks a question.

Example   That was a great game said Jim.

Step 1: Identify the words that Jim said. Underline the words.

<u>That was a great game</u> said Jim.

Step 2: Put quotation marks around those words.

"That was a great game" said Jim.

Step 3: Place a comma inside the last set of quotation marks to separate the speaker's name from the exact words.

"That was a great game," said Jim.

A Place quotation marks and a comma in these sentences.

1. Rico announced I'm going to join the army.

2. Dinner will be at six said Mrs. Conte.

3. It was not my fault explained Mary.

4. Nancy said I just found ten dollars.

5. Don't stay out too late said Mom.

6. Have you seen my keys asked Dad.

7. They are on the table replied Luis.

8. Alison said Tom asked me to the dance.

9. What will you wear asked Carol.

10. I have a new blue dress replied Alison.

Sometimes the speaker's name is in the middle of a quotation. Put quotation marks around each part of the quotation. Start the second part of the quotation with a small letter if the same sentence is in both parts. Start the second part of the quotation with a capital letter if it starts a new sentence. Put a comma after the first part of the quotation and after the speaker's name. Put end punctuation at the end of the second part. The end punctuation goes inside the quotation marks.

Example   After dinner said Joe I am going to the mall.

Step 1: Identify the words Joe said. Underline the words.

<u>After dinner</u> said Joe <u>**I am going to the mall**</u>.

Step 2: Put quotation marks around both parts of the underlined words.

"After dinner" said Joe "I am going to the mall."

Step 3: Place commas to separate each part of the quotation from the speaker's name.

"After dinner," said Joe, "I am going to the mall."

B Put quotation marks and commas in these sentences.

1. No said Paul I did not buy a car.

2. I found this bone said Ken buried in the yard.

3. I think said Tiko it is going to rain today.

4. Yes replied Ed I have finished my homework.

5. This bike said Carl belongs to George.

6. Do you know asked Fred where I can find Will?

7. That telephone exclaimed Bud never stops ringing!

8. My little sister said Alex is waiting for me.

9. Today announced Pat is my sixteenth birthday.

10. Yes the clerk said we have that CD.

LESSON 7　Direct and Indirect Quotations

KEY WORDS

Direct quotation
the exact words
a person said

Indirect quotation
a description of what
a person said that is
not the speaker's exact
words; often introduced
by the word *that*

A **direct quotation** is the exact words that a speaker said. Quotation marks are placed around a direct quotation. An **indirect quotation** tells what the speaker has said but does not use the speaker's exact words. An indirect quotation does not need quotation marks. Commas are not needed to set off the speaker's name in indirect quotations.

Example　Jon said that he likes to play golf.

Guy said I like golf, too!

Step 1: Look at the first sentence. The word *that* shows you it is not Jon's exact words.

Jon said **that** he likes to play golf. ◄— An indirect quotation often starts with *that*.

The sentence contains an indirect quotation. It tells you what Jon said but not in his exact words. No quotation marks or commas are needed.

Step 2: Look at the second sentence. Does it note Guy's exact words? Yes. Underline Guy's words.

Guy said <u>I like golf, too!</u> ◄———— These are Guy's exact words.

Step 3: The sentence contains a direct quotation. Place quotation marks around Guy's words. Place a comma after *said*.

Guy said, "I like golf, too!"

A Read each sentence. Write *IQ* on the line if the sentence contains an indirect quotation. Place quotation marks and a comma where needed if the sentence contains a direct quotation.

1. Mae said I have to buy a birthday present for Tiko. _____

2. Ross said that he would wait for me by the front door. _____

3. Kia told me that she was looking for a job. _____

4. Who wants to go bowling asked Kyle. _____

5. Mike thinks that the book belongs to Jim. _____

6. I told Sue that I could not give her a ride. _____

7. Nate said that Dan would be late for the meeting. _____

8. My dog ate my homework explained Ruth. _____

9. Did you see my sister asked Carl. _____

10. Emma said that her family is moving to Florida. _____

You can change an **indirect quotation** to a direct quotation. If the indirect quotation contains *that,* remove it. Then change *he, she,* or *they* to *I* or *we.* Place quotation marks, capital letters, and commas where needed.

| **Example** | Jill and Donna said that they are going to the beach. |

Step 1: Remove *that* from the sentence.

Jill and Donna said ~~that~~ they are going to the beach.

Step 2: Change the pronoun *they* to *we* to show that Jill and Donna are talking about themselves.

Jill and Donna said **we** are going to the beach.

Step 3: Place quotation marks around the direct quotation. Insert a comma after *said.* Capitalize *we.*

Jill and Donna said, "**We** are going to the beach."

B **Change each indirect quotation to a direct quotation. Write the new sentence on the line.**

1. My boss said that she will hire another worker.

_____

_____

2. Russ said that algebra is a hard subject.

_____

_____

3. Ed said that the concert was great!

_____

_____

4. My father said that he will buy a car

_____

_____

5. Ida said that red is a beautiful color.

_____

_____

LESSON 8   Kinds of Sentences

KEY WORDS

Declarative sentence
a sentence that states
a fact and ends with
a period

**Interrogative
sentence**
a sentence that asks
a question and ends
with a question mark

Imperative sentence
a sentence that gives
a command and ends
with a period

**Exclamatory
sentence**
a sentence that
expresses strong
feeling and ends with
an exclamation point

There are four kinds of sentences. A **declarative sentence** makes a statement. It ends with a period. An **interrogative sentence** asks a question. It ends with a question mark. An **imperative sentence** gives a command or makes a request. It usually ends with a period. Sometimes it ends with an exclamation point. An **exclamatory sentence** shows strong feelings. It ends with an exclamation point.

Example   Take out the garbage, Jack.

Step 1: Decide on the message of the sentence.

Take out the garbage, Jack. ◄— The sentence makes a request of Jack.

Step 2: Review the key words. What kind of sentence makes a request or gives a command?

Take out the garbage, Jack. ◄—The purpose of an imperative sentence is to make a request or give a command.

The purpose of the sentence is to give a **command**.

A Write the purpose of each sentence on the line. Choose from the following: *Statement   Question   Command   Exclamatory*

1. Are you going to the dance on Saturday?   _____

2. That was the best movie I ever saw!   _____

3. Yesterday was my birthday.   _____

4. Get off my car.   _____

5. Please wash the board.   _____

6. Sam left for soccer practice.   _____

7. Did you ever see the Grand Canyon?   _____

8. Tell me everything you know about Mexico.   _____

9. Thomas Jefferson was the third president.   _____

10. Why did you call your mother?   _____

B More practice. Write four sentences about the first day of school. Write one declarative sentence, one interrogative sentence, one imperative sentence, and one exclamatory sentence.

1. Declarative sentence

_____

_____

_____

_____

2. Interrogative sentence

_____

_____

_____

_____

3. Imperative sentence

_____

_____

_____

_____

4. Exclamatory sentence

_____

_____

_____

C More practice. Write four sentences about friendship. Write one declarative sentence, one interrogative sentence, one imperative sentence, and one exclamatory sentence.

1. Declarative _____

2. Interrogative _____

3. Imperative _____

4. Exclamatory _____

UNIT TEST

Part 1
Matching Definitions

Match each word in Column A with its definition in Column B.

Column A	Column B
____ **1.** Comma	**A.** part of a sentence that tells who or what the sentence is about
____ **2.** Declarative sentence	**B.** gives a command and ends with a period
____ **3.** Direct quotation	**C.** part of a sentence that tells about the subject; always has a verb
____ **4.** End punctuation	**D.** punctuation mark used to separate words or groups of words
____ **5.** Exclamatory sentence	**E.** marks placed at the beginning and end of a direct quotation
____ **6.** Imperative sentence	**F.** period, question mark, or exclamation point
____ **7.** Interrogative sentence	**G.** word that shows action or a state of being
____ **8.** Predicate	**H.** group of words that expresses a complete thought
____ **9.** Quotation marks	**I.** expresses strong feeling and ends with an exclamation point
____ **10.** Subject	**J.** a speaker's exact words
____ **11.** Sentence	**K.** asks a question and ends with a question mark
____ **12.** Verb	**L.** states a fact and ends with a period

Part 2
Identifying Sentences

Write *S* if the group of words is a sentence.
Write *F* if the group of words is a sentence fragment.

1. After the sudden rainstorm. _____

2. Take out the trash. _____

3. Emma jogged around the track. _____

4. Before the play begins. _____

5. Many cars on the highway. _____

Part 3
Subjects and Predicates

Circle the subject in each sentence. Underline the predicate.

1. Mel Gibson is my favorite actor.

2. Tia works at a movie theater.

3. A sleek sports car sped down the street.

4. The cranky baby cried all afternoon.

5. _____
The soccer team has practice on Saturday.

**Part 4
Beginning and
Ending Sentences**

Find the four sentences in the paragraph. List them on the lines. Capitalize the first word in each sentence. Use an end punctuation mark at the end of each sentence.

liz works out each week she eats a balanced diet she gets eight hours of sleep each night liz practices good health habits

1. _____

2. _____

3. _____

4. _____

**Part 5
Commas**

Put commas where needed in each sentence.

1. Sue Jon and Bev live in Belleville Illinois.

2. Mrs. Dixon washed dried and folded the clothes.

3. Mica was born on October 29 1985 in Macon Georgia.

4. My classmates collected canned goods packed them in boxes and put the boxes on the truck.

5. Would you prefer coffee tea milk or juice with your meal?

**Part 6
Quotations**

If the sentence contains a direct quotation, put quotation marks and a comma where needed. If the sentence contains an indirect quotation, write *IQ* on the line.

1. Yes said Jim I passed my driving test. _____

2. You may leave when the bell rings said the teacher. _____

3. Nancy said that the movie was funny. _____

4. This story explained Mr. Wall is about a Civil War hero. _____

5. Les told me that the picnic starts at noon. _____

**Part 7
Kinds of Sentences**

Read each sentence. Write the kind of sentence each one is on the line. Choose from the following: *Declarative, Exclamatory, Interrogative,* or *Imperative.* Put the correct end punctuation after the last word.

1. Have you seen Mr. Walters today _____

2. Hang up your coat _____

3. This cake is delicious _____

4. Abby missed the bus this morning _____

5. Are you running for class president _____

LESSON 9   What Is a Noun?

KEY WORDS

Noun
a word that names a
person, place, thing,
or idea

Collective noun
a word that names
a group of people
or things

Compound noun
a noun that is more
than one word

A **noun** is a word that names a person, place, thing, or idea.

Example My brother bought pants and a shirt at the mall.

Step 1: Find the words that name a person, place, thing, or idea.

My **brother** bought **pants** and a **shirt** at the **mall**.

Person   Thing   Place

Step 2: Underline the nouns in the sentence.

My <u>brother</u> bought <u>pants</u> and a <u>shirt</u> at the <u>mall</u>.

A Underline the nouns in each sentence.

1. Tim caught three fish at the lake.

2. Edie put the pie in the oven.

3. My dog hid his bone under the sofa.

4. The award brought Mark great joy.

5. Paula works as a nurse in the hospital.

6. Did the waiter take your order?

7. My sister dropped her keys on the table.

8. I found your book in the hallway.

9. Do you want milk or juice with your sandwich?

10. What is the capital of Texas?

A **collective noun** is a word that names a group of people or things.

Example The crowd cheered for their favorite team.

Step 1: Find the words that name a group of people or things.

The **crowd** cheered for their favorite **team**.

Group of People

Step 2: Underline the collective nouns.

The <u>crowd</u> cheered for their favorite <u>team</u>.

B Underline the collective nouns in each sentence.

RULES TO REMEMBER

■ A collective noun names one group made up of more than one part.

■ Compound words may be connected by a hyphen between the words. Some are written as one word. Some are written as two or more separate words.

1. A flock of geese flew over our house.

2. A work crew cleaned up the park after the crowd left.

3. The band performed for its audience.

4. Members of my family live in different parts of the country.

5. Sam has a collection of leaves from the trees in our yard.

6. A swarm of bees rested on the soda cans.

7. The swim team is getting ready for a series of meets.

8. That group of people is a jury.

9. The Fitness Club bought a set of exercise equipment.

10. The crowd of swimmers watched a school of fish float by.

A **compound noun** is a noun that is more than one word. Some compound nouns are joined by a hyphen. Some are two separate words. Some compound nouns are written as one word.

Example | Do you go to the high school on Oak Street?

Step 1: Find the nouns that are formed from two or more words joined together.

Do you go to the **high school** on **Oak Street**?

Two words name one place.

Step 2: Underline the compound nouns in the sentence.

Do you go to the **high school** on **Oak Street**?

C Underline the compound nouns in the sentences.

1. Elie bought a new television set for her living room.

2. I brought hot dogs and watermelon to the picnic.

3. Rico left his backpack at the bus stop.

4. My brother-in-law works at Town Hall.

5. The police chief is waiting in the backyard.

6. Did you get those French fries in the dining hall?

7. A clump of ice cream fell on my new sweatshirt.

8. The Vice-Principal took Mike's cell phone.

9. Liz threw an old toothbrush into the trashcan.

10. My pen pal attends high school in London, England.

LESSON 10   Common and Proper Nouns

KEY WORDS

Common noun
the name of any person, place, thing, or idea

Proper noun
the name of a specific person, place, thing, or idea

A **common noun** is a word that names any person, place, thing, or idea. A **proper noun** names a specific person, place, thing, or idea. A proper noun begins with a capital letter. Names of languages are proper nouns: *English, Spanish*. Titles are proper nouns: *President Jackson, Lord of the Rings*. Names of subjects are common nouns: *social studies, science*. Names of courses are proper nouns: *Introduction to Biology*.

Example   White House   building   Buckingham Palace

Step 1: Look for the nouns that name a specific person, place, thing, or idea.

White House   building

Building is a common noun.
White House is a specific building. It is a proper noun.

Step 2: Circle the proper noun.

(White House)   building

A Circle the proper noun in each pair of words. Then write another proper noun that could be used for the common noun.

1. state   California   _____
2. holiday   New Year's Eve   _____
3. Mercury   planet   _____
4. day   Thursday   _____
5. book   Where the Wild Things Are _____
6. country   Japan   _____
7. January   month   _____
8. rock group   U2   _____
9. NY Yankees   team   _____
10. actor   Matt Damon   _____

The band will perform in Orlando, Florida next month.

Step 1: Find the words that name a person, place, thing, or idea.

The **band** will perform in **Orlando, Florida** next **month**.

Step 2: Identify which of the words are common nouns. Underline the common nouns.

The **band** will perform in Orlando, Florida next **month**.

Step 3: Identify which of the words are proper nouns. Circle the proper nouns.

The band will perform in Orlando, Florida next month.

B Write the sentences on the lines. Underline the common nouns. Capitalize the proper nouns.

1. My favorite actor is mel gibson.

_____

2. Dee drove to her home in jacksonville, florida.

_____

3. On tuesday, Ben will move to 35 main street, oakville, new york.

_____

4. I sent Jennifer a postcard from dublin, ireland.

_____

5. The 2002 winter olympics were held in salt lake city, utah.

_____

6. On wednesday, adam starts classes at the university of miami.

_____

7. Have you ever visited the statue of liberty?

_____

8. I am writing a report about the planets earth and venus.

_____

9. The capital of new jersey is trenton.

_____

10. Is your birthday in may or july?

_____

LESSON 11   Singular and Plural Nouns

KEY WORDS

Singular noun
the name of one person, place, thing, or idea

Plural noun
the name of more than one person, place, thing, or idea

Consonant
all the letters of the alphabet that are not vowels

Vowel
these letters of the alphabet: *a, e, i, o, u,* and sometimes *y*

A **singular noun** is the name of one person, place, thing, or idea. A **plural noun** is the name of more than one person, place, thing, or idea. You can make many singular nouns plural by adding *-s.*

Example   My dog hid the bone in the yard.

Step 1: Find the words that name a person, place, thing, or idea. Underline the singular nouns.

My **dog** hid the **bone** in the **yard**.

Step 2: Write the plural form of each noun by adding *-s.*

Singular	Plural
dog	dog**s**
bone	bone**s**
yard	yard**s**

A Underline the singular nouns in the sentence. Then write the plural form of each noun on the line.

1. The player hit a baseball over the fence. _____

2. My sister bought an apple, banana, and orange at the store. _____

3. Did you ask your neighbor to the dance? _____

4. My aunt is a doctor in that hospital. _____

5. A jet flew over the crowd at the Air Show. _____

Sometimes you must add more than *-s* to make a singular noun plural. Add *-es* to form the plural if a singular noun ends in *s, z, x, ch,* or *sh.*

Example   Put your lunch on this dish.

Step 1: Find the words that name a person, place, thing, or idea. Underline the singular nouns.

Put your **lunch** on this **dish**.

Step 2: Write the plural form of each noun by adding -es.

Singular	Plural
lunch	lunch**es**
dish	dish**es**

B Underline the singular nouns in the sentence. Then write the plural form of each noun on the line.

1. The singer practiced her song before lunch. _____

2. Alice put the watch inside a box. _____

3. Every worker must pay tax to the government. _____

4. Dale cut a rose from the bush in her garden. _____

5. The clerk put a new tag on the dress. _____

There are special rules to follow when making a word that ends with y plural. Add -s to form the plural if the letter before the y is a **vowel**. If the letter before the y is a **consonant**, change the y to i and then add -es to form the plural.

Example | I spent my birthday at a party in the city.

Step 1: Find the words that name a person, place, idea, or thing. Underline the singular nouns.

I spent my **birthday** at a **party** in the **city**.

Step 2: Write the plural form of each noun.

Singular		Plural
birthday	← Just add -s →	**birthdays**
party	Change y to i	**parties**
city	Then add -es	**cities**

C Write the plural form of each noun on the line.

1. monkey _____

2. lady _____

3. holiday _____

4. ray _____

5. baby _____

6. toy _____

7. story _____

8. puppy _____

9. turkey _____

10. French fry _____

LESSON 12   Possessive Nouns

KEY WORDS

Possessive noun
a noun that shows ownership or a relationship between two things

Apostrophe
a punctuation mark (') that shows a noun is possessive

A **possessive noun** shows ownership. It can also show a relationship between two things. A possessive noun always has a punctuation mark called an **apostrophe**. Singular nouns usually show possession by adding an apostrophe plus an -s.

Example   What is the possessive noun in this sentence?

I put Anne's sweater on the chair.

Step 1: Find the word that has an apostrophe. Underline the possessive noun.

I put **Anne's** sweater on the chair.

Step 2: Describe the relationship between Anne and the sweater.

I put <u>Anne's</u> sweater on the chair.   **The sweater belongs to Anne.**

A Underline the possessive noun in each sentence. Then describe the relationship it shows.

1. Did you find Todd's keys?

_____

2. My brother's car was stolen.

_____

3. I heard Rita's phone ringing.

_____

4. Where is the dog's leash?

_____

5. A nail is stuck in the bicycle's tire.

_____

B More Practice. Write the possessive form of each singular noun on the line.

1. teacher _____

2. student _____

3. mother _____

4. baby _____

5. judge _____

6. boss _____

7. actor _____

8. puppy _____

9. class _____

10. winner _____

A plural noun can show ownership, too. When a plural noun ends in s, place an apostrophe at the end of the word. This will make it a possessive noun. When a plural noun does not end in s, add an apostrophe and -s to make it a possessive noun.

Example   children   clerks

Look at the last letter in each word. If the word ends in s, add an apostrophe. If the last letter is not an s, add apostrophe and –s.

children	clerks
Ends in -n	Ends in -s
Add 's	Add '
children's	clerks'

C Write the possessive form of each plural noun on the line.

1. workers _____

2. women _____

3. parents _____

4. farmers _____

5. mice _____

6. horses _____

7. kittens _____

8. painters _____

9. ladies _____

10. teams _____

LESSON 13   What Is a Pronoun?

KEY WORDS

Pronoun
a word that
replaces a noun

Antecedent
the noun that a
pronoun replaces

A **pronoun** is a word that takes the place of a noun. An **antecedent** is the noun that a pronoun replaces. *I, you, he, she, we, they, me, him, her, us, them,* and *their* are examples of pronouns.

> **Example**   What are the pronoun and antecedent in this sentence?
>
> Dave was glad that he had brought a drink to practice.
>
> **Step 1:** Find the pronoun in the sentence. Underline the pronoun.
>
> Dave was glad that **he** had brought a drink to practice.
>
> **Step 2:** Find the noun that the pronoun *he* replaces. It is the antecedent. Write the antecedent on the line.
>
> **Dave** was glad that <u>he</u> had brought a drink to practice.   **Dave**

A Underline the pronouns in each sentence. Write the antecedents on the line. Some sentences will have more than one antecedent.

1. Jean and Barb are sisters, and they attend the same school. _____
   _____

2. Paolo said that he would call his coach. _____
   _____

3. Aaron wrote a story about his trip to New York City. _____
   _____

4. Carol and I are on the same team, so we practice together. _____
   _____

5. Zack bought some flowers, and he gave them to Alison. _____
   _____

6. Since Joan and Ed are neighbors, they ride home together. _____
   _____

7. Mike said that he gave the book to June. _____
   _____

8. Dee and Al wrote their report, and they gave it to Mrs. Dixon. _____
_____

9. Since she lost weight, Ann got rid of her old clothes. _____
_____

10. Larry was thrilled that his team won the game. _____
_____

11. Rico and I bought a gift for our teacher. _____
_____

12. Jeff thought that he had lost his backpack. _____
_____

13. Where did Ellen park her car? _____
_____

14. Luis and I went to the mall, but we did not find Beth. _____
_____

15. Mr. Daniels thought that he had mailed the letter. _____
_____

B More Practice. Find the ten pronouns in the paragraph. List them in order on the lines. Write the antecedent next to each one.

Bev and Ed like to ski. They go almost every week. Ed said that he knew how to ski before he knew how to walk. Bev did not start skiing until she was twelve. She learned the sport from Ed. She says that he was a very good teacher. Now when they have a downhill race, she always beats him!

1. _____   **6.** _____

2. _____   **7.** _____

3. _____   **8.** _____

4. _____   **9.** _____

5. _____   **10.** _____

LESSON 14   Personal Pronouns

KEY WORDS

Personal pronoun
a pronoun that refers to a person or thing

First-person pronoun
a pronoun that refers to the person who is speaking

Second-person pronoun
a pronoun that refers to the person who is being spoken to

Third-person pronoun
a pronoun that refers to the person or thing that is being talked about

A **personal pronoun** takes the place of a noun that names a person or thing. A **first-person** pronoun refers to the person who is speaking. *I, me, my,* and *mine* are all singular first-person pronouns.

Example   Underline the first-person pronouns in these sentences.

Today I bought my first car. My father helped me pick it out. As I drove home, I still could not believe it was mine!

Today **I** bought **my** first car. **My** father helped **me** pick it out. As **I** drove home, **I** still could not believe it was **mine**!

A Underline the first-person pronouns in the paragraph.

Yesterday was the best day of my life. I discovered I had made the cheerleading squad. Friends of mine saw the list first. They grabbed me from the lunchroom and took me to the office. I was shocked to see my name.

Some first-person pronouns are plural. *We, us, our,* and *ours* are plural first-person pronouns.

B Find the first-person pronouns in the paragraph. List all eleven of them on the lines.

After school, we had a celebration. We went to our favorite ice cream shop. Each of us ordered a huge sundae. The waitress did not think we would finish our treats. But we made sure our bowls were empty. I hope I can fit into my cheerleading outfit.

Singular _____ _____ _____

_____ _____ _____

_____ _____ _____

Plural _____ _____ _____

_____ _____ _____

_____ _____ _____

Second-person pronouns refer to the person being spoken to. *You, your,* and *yours* are all second-person pronouns.

| **Example** | Underline the second-person pronouns in this sentence. |

Did you find your notebook?

Did **you** find **your** notebook?

C Underline the second-person pronouns in the sentences.

1. When will you be ready to go?

2. Did you give your report to Mr. Scott?

3. You should not chew gum in school.

4. Did Jon ask you for your phone number?

5. What is your e-mail address?

Third-person pronouns refer to the person or thing that is being talked about. *He, him, his, she, her, hers, it, its, they, them, their,* and *theirs* are third-person pronouns.

D Find the ten third-person pronouns in the paragraph. List them in order on the lines. Write the antecedent next to each one.

Rachel and Ryan are twins. Their parents decided to surprise them with a puppy. The parents waited until the kids were at school to bring it home. Rachel screamed when she saw the puppy. Her eyes filled with tears. She was delighted. Ryan's eyes filled with tears, too. He was not so happy about the puppy. He saw that it had chewed on his autographed baseball.

1. _____   **6.** _____

2. _____   **7.** _____

3. _____   **8.** _____

4. _____   **9.** _____

5. _____   **10.** _____

RULES TO REMEMBER

■ First-person pronouns refer to the speaker. *I, me, my, we, us, our, ours,* and *mine* are first-person pronouns.

■ Second-person pronouns refer to the person who is spoken to. *You, your,* and *yours* are second-person pronouns.

■ Third-person pronouns refer to the person or thing being talked about. *He, him, his, she, her, hers, it, its, they, them, their,* and *theirs* are third-person pronouns.

LESSON 15   Relative Pronouns

A **relative pronoun** shows a relationship. The relationship is between the pronoun and the antecedent. *Who, whom,* and *whose* are relative pronouns that refer to people. *Which* and *what* are relative pronouns that refer to things. *That* is a relative pronoun that refers to either people or things.

Example   Find the relative pronoun and antecedent in this sentence.

Jane wants to borrow the dress that Mia bought last week.

Step 1:   Find the word that refers to a person or thing. Underline the relative pronoun.

Jane wants to borrow the dress **that** Mia bought last week.

Step 2:   Find the word that the pronoun that refers to. It is the antecedent. Write the antecedent on the line.

Jane wants to borrow the **dress** that Mia bought last week.

dress

 Underline the relative pronoun in each sentence.
Write the antecedent on the line.

1. Tony's car, which is blue, is parked in the lot.

_____

2. The dinner that Sue made was delicious.

_____

3. Jed's brother, who is a teacher, helped me study for the test.

_____

4. Rick has a friend whose mother is an artist.

_____

5. Did you see the report that I just printed?

_____

Combining a relative pronoun with the word *ever* forms a **compound relative pronoun**. *Whoever, whomever, whichever,* and *whatever* are compound relative pronouns. *Whoever* and *whomever* refer to people. *Whichever* and *whatever* refer to things. The antecedent of these pronouns is not stated. The antecedent is a group of people or things the listener already knows.

| **Example** | Find the compound relative pronoun in this sentence. Underline the compound relative pronoun.

"Help yourself to whatever you want," said the host.

Find the relative pronoun with the word *ever*. Underline it.

"Help yourself to **whatever** you want," said the host.

Whatever is the compound relative pronoun. It refers to a thing or things.

B **Underline the compound relative pronouns in each sentence.**

1. Whoever owns that dog should make him stop barking.

2. Please give whatever you can to the food bank.

3. You may borrow whichever of these CDs you want.

4. Ted will ask whomever he wants to the dance.

5. Whoever wrote this note has sloppy handwriting.

C **More Practice. Underline the correct pronoun in each sentence.**

1. This is the boy (which, whose) book I borrowed.

2. The quilt (whom, that) Aida made is beautiful.

3. Choose (whatever, whomever) kind of ice cream you want.

4. Eric has a friend (that, who) is a member of the band.

5. Where is the girl (whom, which) you met at camp?

LESSON 16   Interrogative Pronouns

KEY WORDS

Interrogative pronoun
a pronoun that introduces a question

An **interrogative pronoun** is a word that introduces a question. The interrogative pronouns are *who, whom, whose, which,* and *what. Who* and *whom* refer to a person or persons. *Whose* shows possession. *What* refers to things, places, or ideas. *Which* refers to people or things. *Which* also is used when the answer is a choice between two or more things.

Example

Choose the correct interrogative pronoun in this sentence.

(Which, What) girls made the team?

Step 1: Review the information about interrogative pronouns:

What refers to things, places, and ideas.

Which refers to people or things. *Which* is also used when the answer is a choice between two or more people or things.

Step 2: Ask yourself what the interrogative pronoun in this sentence is referring to.

(Which, What) **girls** made the team? The interrogative pronoun refers to *girls.*

Step 3: Underline the correct interrogative pronoun.

(<u>**Which**</u>, What) girls made the team?

 Underline the correct interrogative pronoun in each sentence.

1. Amy asked (which, who) of the girls is my sister.

2. (Whose, Who) knows the combination to this lock?

3. (Whose, What) kind of music do you like?

4. (Which, What) of these CDs belongs to you?

5. Mark asked (who, whose) car is parked outside.

6. Tell me (which, what) you want to know.

7. (Which, What) of these jackets do you like best?

8. Rico asked for (whose, whom) am I buying a gift.

9. Do you know (which, whom) team won the game?

10. (Which, What) is the capital of Texas?

Sometimes using *who* and *whom* can be confusing. Both words are interrogative pronouns. Use *who* when the sentence needs a subject pronoun. For example, *Who* is the teacher? Use *whom* when the sentence already has a subject and needs an objective pronoun. For example, *Whom* did you invite? To test the correct choice at the beginning of a question, turn the question into a statement. *(You did invite whom.)* If the statement has a subject, use *whom*.

Example   Choose the correct interrogative pronoun in this sentence.

Molly wanted to know (who, whom) I went hiking with.

Step 1: Decide whether the sentence needs a subject pronoun.

Molly wanted to know (who, whom) I went hiking with. The sentence already has a subject. It does not need a subject pronoun.

Step 2: Underline the correct interrogative pronoun.

Molly wanted to know (who, **whom**) I went hiking with.

B **Underline the correct interrogative pronoun in each sentence.**

1. (Who, Whom) are you talking to?

2. (Who, Whom) is going to the mall?

3. To (who, whom) are you writing?

4. (Who, Whom) is taking French next semester?

5. For (who, whom) did you write that song?

6. (Who, Whom) was at the game last night?

7. (Who, Whom) has already had strep throat?

8. Rachel wants to know with (who, whom) you are going to the prom.

9. For (who, whom) are you buying flowers?

10. (Who, Whom) is playing out of tune?

LESSON 17   Demonstrative Pronouns

KEY WORDS

Demonstrative pronoun
a pronoun that points to nouns: *this, these, that,* and *those*

A **demonstrative pronoun** points out a noun. The demonstrative pronouns are *this, these, that,* and *those*. *This* and *that* are singular. They refer to one person or thing. *These* and *those* are plural. They refer to more than one person or thing.

Example Find the demonstrative pronoun in this sentence. Then identify the noun the demonstrative pronoun points out.

Is that your backpack by the bus?

Step 1: Underline the demonstrative pronoun.

Is **that** your backpack by the bus?

Step 2: Circle the noun the demonstrative pronoun points out.

Is that your (backpack) by the bus?

A Underline the demonstrative pronoun in each sentence. Circle the noun it points out.

1. Is this the book you are looking for?

2. Those papers on the desk belong to Tom.

3. These are my parents.

4. Is that the school you attend?

5. Are those Nate's sneakers?

6. This is my cell phone.

7. Did you see that girl by the door?

8. Those people across the street are my neighbors.

9. Are these your gloves?

10. Is this your new CD?

11. Put that empty bottle in the trash.

12. Leave those clothes near the washing machine.

13. Is that the girl who called you?

14. Are these flowers from your garden?

15. I made this dinner just for you.

B More practice. Underline the correct demonstrative pronoun in each sentence

1. (This, These) is my new computer.

2. Is (that, those) your mother in the car?

3. Are (this, these) your coins?

4. Where are (that, those) sounds coming from?

5. (This, These) is the dress I bought yesterday.

6. (This, These) are the books we have to read this summer.

7. (That, Those) baby just dropped her doll.

8. Are (that, those) Guy's parents at the door?

9. (This, These) is the field where we will play our game.

10. Where are (that, those) stamps you just bought?

C More practice. Write a sentence using each demonstrative pronoun.

1. this _____

2. these _____

3. that_____

4. those_____

LESSON 18 Indefinite Pronouns

KEY WORDS

Indefinite pronoun
a pronoun that refers
to a noun that is not
named

An **indefinite pronoun** does not refer to a specific person or thing. An indefinite pronoun does not have a clear antecedent. Most indefinite pronouns are singular. A few are plural. The chart below lists some common indefinite pronouns:

Singular			Plural
another	everybody	one	all
anybody	everyone	one another	both
any one	everything	somebody	few
anything	neither	someone	many
each	nobody	something	several
each other	no one		some
either	nothing		others

Example Look at the chart above. Then find and underline the indefinite pronoun in this sentence.

Someone is tapping on the window.

Someone does not name who is tapping on the window. *Someone* is the indefinite pronoun.

<u>**Someone**</u> is tapping on the window.

 Underline the indefinite pronoun in each sentence.

1. Does anything ever bother you?

2. Several of my classmates failed the test.

3. Lynn said that everyone is going to the meeting.

4. Neither of us wants to go bowling.

5. Many of the band members take music lessons.

6. All of the players scored a goal.

7. Several of the fans jumped onto the field.

8. Tina and Bill said good-bye to each other.

9. Both of my parents speak Spanish.

10. Someone should call the police.

11. Is something wrong with Mr. Diaz?

12. Nobody knows Mrs. Hall's address.

13. Everybody seems ready for vacation.

14. Has anyone called Beth?

15. Nothing went wrong today!

Most indefinite pronouns are singular. A few are plural. A singular indefinite pronoun refers to one person or thing. A plural indefinite pronoun refers to more than one person or thing.

> **Example** Find the indefinite pronoun in this sentence. Then underline the indefinite pronoun. Write whether it is *singular* or *plural*.
>
> Both of the actors are in my English class.
>
> Since *actors* is plural, a plural indefinite pronoun is needed.
>
> **Both** of the actors are in my English class.   **Plural**

B Underline the indefinite pronoun in each sentence. Write *singular* or *plural* on the line.

1. Many of the teachers walk to school.   _____

2. Several of the nurses have gotten sick.   _____

3. Somebody rings the bell every morning.   _____

4. Both of the workers need computers.   _____

5. All of the children took their crayons.   _____

6. Do you know anyone here?   _____

7. The nurse weighed many of the students.   _____

8. Neither of us likes this dessert.   _____

9. Everyone knows the capital of New York.   _____

10. Few of the flowers were white.   _____

UNIT TEST

Part 1
Matching Definitions

Match each word in Column A with its definition in Column B.

Column A	Column B
____ **1.** Antecedent	**A.** two or more words joined together to form one new noun
____ **2.** Apostrophe	**B.** word that names a person, place, thing, or idea
____ **3.** Collective noun	**C.** name of more than one person, place, thing, or idea
____ **4.** Common noun	**D.** name of a group of people, places, or things
____ **5.** Compound noun	**E.** word that shows ownership or a relationship between two things
____ **6.** Noun	**F.** word that takes the place of a noun
____ **7.** Plural noun	**G.** name of a particular person, place, thing, or idea
____ **8.** Possessive noun	**H.** noun that a pronoun replaces
____ **9.** Pronoun	**I.** punctuation mark that shows a noun is possessive
____**10.** Proper noun	**J.** name of any person, place, thing, or idea

Part 2
Identifying Nouns

Underline the nouns in these sentences.

1. Emily went to the park after school.

2. Alice bought a television set for her bedroom.

3. Dana made spaghetti and meatballs for dinner.

4. The puppy hid under a chair in the living room.

5. Lisa has the lead role in the play.

Part 3
Common and Proper Nouns

Underline the common nouns in the sentences. Circle the proper nouns that should be capitalized.

1. My brother teaches english at wilson high school.

2. Lee visited new york city and saw the statue of liberty.

3. In september, marie will take classes at the university of arizona.

4. Beth stopped in jacksonville, florida during her tour of the south.

5. Russ spent new year's day in houston, texas.

Part 4
Plural Nouns

Circle the plural nouns in these sentences.

1. The children ate hot dogs and hamburgers at the picnic.

2. Nate discovered five mice hiding under the leaves.

3. Mayor Brown has given a dozen speeches this month.

4. The students are writing reports on the countries of South America.

5. Bob scored ten goals in his soccer matches.

Part 5
Possessive Nouns

Underline the possessive nouns in these sentences.

1. Jim's shoes are in the men's locker room.

2. My neighbor's cat is sitting under Juan's car.

3. Do you have Carl's keys?

4. Mr. Ruiz hung Ed's painting in the school's main office.

5. Students are not allowed to park in the teachers' lot.

Part 6
Personal Pronouns

Underline the personal pronouns in each sentence. Write the antecedents on the line.

1. Sue put her backpack on the desk. _____

2. Where did my mother park our car?_____

3. Max said that he would call my parents. _____

4. Carol and Joe made a video about their trip to Florida. _____

5. Since we finished our homework, Ben and I are going out.

_____

Part 7
Other Kinds of Pronouns

Circle the pronoun in each sentence. Write the kind of pronoun each one is on the line. Choose from the following: *Relative, Interrogative, Demonstrative,* or *Indefinite*.

1. Whom did Tom ask to the dance? _____

2. Everybody cheered for the team. _____

3. The dress that Dee wore was beautiful! _____

4. Zack called a girl who is in my class._____

5. That is my sweatshirt! _____

LESSON 19   **What Is an Adjective?**

Adjective
a word that describes
or tells about a noun
or pronoun

Predicate adjective
an adjective that comes
after the noun or
pronoun it describes

An **adjective** is a word that describes or tells about a noun or pronoun. An adjective may tell *what kind, which one, how many,* or *how much.* An adjective usually comes before the noun or pronoun it describes.

Example   Find the adjective in this sentence.

Nathan won a gold medal for his project.

Step 1: Find the word that describes a noun or pronoun. Underline the adjective.

Nathan won a **gold** medal for his project.

Step 2: What noun does the adjective *gold* describe? Write the noun on the line.

Nathan won a gold **medal** for this project.   **medal**

A Underline the adjective in each sentence. Write the noun or pronoun it describes on the line.

1. Ann lost her yellow jacket. _____

2. Did you meet the new teacher? _____

3. Nick made a tasty lunch for us._____

4. We hiked along a dusty trail. _____

5. Don't sit on the broken chair! _____

6. A colorful rainbow crossed the sky. _____

7. Les told the class a funny joke. _____

8. The sweater matches my green pants. _____

9. Angry waves crashed onto the beach._____

10. Sue's ring glistened in the bright sunlight. _____

11. Mia read three books last month._____

12. Can I borrow five dollars? _____

13. I hung the wet bathing suits on the clothesline. _____

14. My frisky kitten tore the curtain. _____

15. Frank enjoyed a glass of cold milk. _____

Most adjectives come *before* the noun or pronoun they describe.
A **predicate adjective** is an adjective that comes *after* the noun or pronoun it describes.

Example   Find the predicate adjective in this sentence.

Bud is nervous about his interview.

Step 1: Look for the word that describes something. Underline the word.

Bud is **nervous** about his interview.

Step 2: Look for the noun that the word *nervous* describes. Write the noun on the line.

Bud is nervous about his interview.   **Bud**

B Underline the predicate adjective in each sentence.
Write the noun or pronoun it describes on the line.

1. Rita was excited about the dance. _____

2. The players are disappointed with the score. _____

3. My milk tastes sour. _____

4. The weather is perfect for a picnic. _____

5. Jon is worried about the test. _____

6. Coach Scott was pleased with the game. _____

7. These cookies are delicious. _____

8. My puppy seems tired today. _____

9. Bart was thrilled with his present. _____

10. The flowers smell sweet. _____

11. Willa's painting is beautiful. _____

12. Dan's speech was interesting. _____

13. The baby was rested after his nap. _____

14. The grass was moist with dew. _____

15. My parents are delighted with my decision. _____

LESSON 20   Articles—A, An, The

KEY WORDS

Definite article
the word *the*; it refers to a specific person, place, thing, or idea

Indefinite article
the words *a* and *an*; they refer to a general group of people, places, things, or ideas

The words *a, an,* and *the* are articles. A **definite article** describes a specific person, place, thing, or idea. The word *the* is a definite article.

Example   Find the definite article in this sentence.

Walt put the report on my desk.

Step 1: Find the article that describes a specific person, place, thing, or idea. Underline the definite article.

Walt put **the** report on my desk.

Step 2: Find the specific thing that *the* describes. Write the noun on the line.

Walt put <u>the</u> **report** on my desk.   **report**

A Underline the definite article in each sentence. Write the noun it describes on the line.

1. Are you going on the class trip? _____

2. We will wait for you in the car. _____

3. Wait until the principal hears this! _____

4. Betty walked along the beach. _____

5. Here is the money I owe you. _____

6. Did you hear the phone ring? _____

7. Claire bought the blue dress. _____

8. The children played in my yard. _____

9. The baseball game is cancelled. _____

10. Please take out the trash. _____

The words *a* and *an* are **indefinite articles**. They are used when talking about a general group of people, places, things, or ideas. The article *a* comes before a word that starts with a consonant. The article *an* comes before a word that starts with a vowel.

Example	Choose the indefinite articles that correctly complete these sentences.

Ron wrote (a, an) story about his trip.
The movie is (a, an) adventure story.

Step 1: If the article comes before a word that starts with a consonant, the article *a* is used. If the article comes before a word that starts with a vowel, the article *an* is used.

Ron wrote (a, an) **s**tory about his trip. ◀────── *Story* starts with a consonant.

The movie is (a, an) **a**dventure story. ◀────── *Adventure* starts with a vowel.

Step 2: Underline the correct indefinite article for each sentence.

Ron wrote (<u>a</u>, an) story about his trip.
The movie is (a, <u>an</u>) adventure story.

B **Underline the indefinite article that correctly completes the sentence.**

1. Who left (a, an) ice pop on the table?

2. Barb made (a, an) apple pie.

3. Jed bought (a, an) computer today.

4. Who left (a, an) note on my car?

5. Put this letter in (a, an) envelope.

6. Leslie has (a, an) gift for you.

7. Would you like (a, an) orange?

8. We are reading (a, an) novel in English class.

9. Does the team have (a, an) game today?

10. Did you send me (a, an) e-mail?

C **More Practice. Underline the article in each sentence. Write *D* on the line if the article is a definite article. Write *I* on the line if the article is an indefinite article.**

1. Where are the keys to my car? _____

2. Tina went to see a movie. _____

3. Do you have an umbrella? _____

4. Tom found a sweatshirt under his bed. _____

5. The police officer gave Mike a ticket for speeding. _____

6. Does your mother work in an office? _____

7. We gave the money to Sal. _____

8. Sharon lost an ice skate. _____

9. Bill rang the doorbell. _____

10. Mae bought a CD from Juan. _____

LESSON 21   Proper Adjectives

KEY WORDS

Proper adjective
the adjective form of
a proper noun

A proper noun names a specific person, place, thing, or idea. You can use a proper noun to describe another noun. This form of a proper noun is called a **proper adjective**. Both proper nouns and proper adjectives are always capitalized.

Example   Find the proper noun that is used as an adjective in this sentence.

The April service project is cleaning up Oak Park.

Step 1: Look for the proper noun that describes another noun. Underline the proper adjective.

The **April** service project is cleaning up Oak Park.

Step 2: Find the noun that the proper adjective describes. Write the noun on the line.

The April **service project** is cleaning up Oak Park.   **service project**

A Underline the proper adjective in each sentence. Write the noun it describes on the line.

1. The store is having a President's Day sale._____

2. Deb bought a set of English china._____

3. Have you eaten at the new Chinese restaurant? _____

4. Sean visited Irish castles on his vacation._____

5. Pat made Belgian waffles for breakfast. _____

6. These shoes are made of Italian leather. _____

7. Claude speaks the French language. _____

8. Did Jon send you a Valentine's Day card? _____

9. Many American athletes won medals at the Olympics. _____

10. Zack brought Danish pastries to the brunch. _____

A proper noun names a specific person, place, thing, or idea. A proper adjective is a proper noun used to describe another noun.

RULES TO REMEMBER

■ A proper adjective describes another noun.

■ Proper nouns and proper adjectives are always capitalized.

Example | There is a proper noun or a proper adjective in each of these sentences. Identify which sentence has a proper noun and which one has a proper adjective.

Two students are learning <u>German</u>.
Both of them are taking a <u>German</u> class.

Step 1: Look at the first sentence. The word *German* does not describe another noun. It is a proper noun. Write *PN* on the line.

Two students are learning <u>German</u>.   **PN**

Step 2: Look at the second sentence. The word *German* describes another noun, so it is a proper adjective. Write the noun it describes on the line.

Both of them are taking a <u>German</u> **class**.   **class**

B Decide whether the underlined word in each sentence is a proper noun or proper adjective. Write *PN* on the line if the word is a proper noun. If the word is a proper adjective, write the noun it describes on the line.

1. Do you like <u>Italian</u> food?_____

2. Jill spent two months in <u>Spain</u>. _____

3. My family is going on a <u>European</u> vacation._____

4. Neha's cousin lives in <u>India</u>._____

5. Our next report is due on <u>Friday</u>._____

6. The band is practicing for the <u>Memorial Day</u> celebration. _____

7. I will be in Bermuda on the <u>Fourth of July</u>._____

8. Larry's birthday is in <u>January</u>._____

9. Tom is studying <u>English</u> literature. _____

10. The <u>October</u> report is due on the fifteenth. _____

LESSON 22   Common Nouns as Adjectives

KEY WORDS

Common noun
a name of any person, place, thing, or idea

Sometimes a **common noun** is used to describe another noun or pronoun. Then the common noun becomes an adjective.

Example   Find the common noun that is used as an adjective in this sentence.

Guy is taking golf lessons.

Step 1: Look for the noun that describes another noun. Underline the noun that is used as an adjective.

Guy is taking **golf** lessons.

Step 2: Write the noun that golf describes on the line.

Guy is taking golf **lessons.**   **lessons**

A **Underline the noun used as an adjective in each sentence. Write the noun it describes on the line.**

1. The players shook hands at center court. _____

2. I spend most summer afternoons at the beach. _____

3. Clyde works at a hardware store. _____

4. Liang is an art teacher. _____

5. Nate put fliers in all the neighborhood mailboxes. _____

6. Paula borrowed my jazz CD. _____

7. A spring snowstorm backed up traffic. _____

8. I will meet you at the movie theater. _____

9. An ocean breeze cooled the sunbathers. _____

10. Dee is shopping for her fall wardrobe. _____

A common noun names any person, place, thing, or idea. A common noun used as an adjective describes another noun or a pronoun. Look closely at how a common noun is used. This will help you decide if it is a noun or an adjective.

Example Are the underlined words in these sentences nouns or adjectives?

The <u>school</u> nurse sent Ed home.

I will wait for Carla in front of the <u>school</u>.

Step 1: Look at the word *school* in the first sentence. It describes the noun that follows it. The word *school* describes *nurse*, so it is an adjective. Write the noun it describes on the line.

The <u>school</u> **nurse** sent Ed home.   **nurse**

Step 2: Look at the word *school* in the second sentence. It does not describe another noun, so it is a common noun. Write *N* on the line.

I will wait for Carla in front of the <u>school</u>.   **N**

B **Decide whether the underlined word in each sentence is a common noun or an adjective. If the word is a common noun, write *N* on the line. If the word is an adjective, write the noun it describes on the line.**

1. Ben rode his bicycle along the <u>dirt</u> road._____

2. Justin teaches an <u>art</u> class after school. _____

3. Ellen will meet us at the <u>mall</u>. _____

4. <u>Summer</u> vacation starts tomorrow. _____

5. My father owns a <u>cleaning</u> business. _____

6. Your sister is waiting in the <u>kitchen</u>. _____

7. We have tickets for the <u>show</u> tonight. _____

8. I heard the <u>boom</u> of thunder in the distance. _____

9. Mae entered a <u>dance</u> contest._____

10. Tiko weeded the <u>flower</u> garden. _____

LESSON 23 Making Comparisons with Adjectives

Adjectives have three forms—the **positive**, the **comparative**, and the **superlative**. All three forms describe or compare nouns. They differ in the number of things that are being compared.

Example

Positive	Comparative	Superlative
fast	faster	fastest
new	newer	newest
kind	kinder	kindest

Decide which adjective is correct in this sentence.

Peter is the (younger, youngest) member of the team.

Step 1: Look at what or who is being compared.
Peter is the (younger, youngest) **member of the team**.

Peter is compared to *team members*.

More than two things are being compared.
Use the superlative form.

Step 2: Underline the superlative adjective.
Peter is the (younger, <u>youngest</u>) member of the team.

A Underline the form of the adjective that is correct in each sentence.

1. Liz is (taller, tallest) than her brother.

2. Tara wore her (new, newer) sweater to the dance.

3. Nate is the (faster, fastest) runner I've ever seen!

4. Ryan throws a baseball (harder, hardest) than Nick.

5. It was (kind, kinder) of you to bring me lunch.

6. Do you know how to change a (flat, flatter) tire?

7. Algebra is the (harder, hardest) class I've ever taken.

8. The red shirt is (big, bigger) than the blue one.

9. Jamie's puppy is (cute, cuter) than my dog.

10. This is the (happier, happiest) day of my life!

Some adjectives have different words for their comparative and superlative forms. The adjectives *good, bad, little,* and *many* are examples of these irregular adjectives.

Example

Positive	Comparative	Superlative
good	better	best
bad	worse	worst

Decide which form of the adjective *good* is correct in these sentences.

Dave is a (good, best) soccer player.
Rico is a (better, best) soccer player than Dave.
Joe is the (best, better) player on the team.

Look at who or what is being compared in each sentence. Then underline the correct form.

Dave is a (<u>good</u>, best) soccer player.

Good describes one noun. Underline the positive form of *good*.

Rico is a (<u>better</u>, best) soccer player than **Dave**.

One person is compared to another. Underline the comparative form of *good*.

Joe is the (<u>best</u>, better) player on the **team**.

More than two players are being compared. Underline the superlative form of *good*.

B Underline the form of the adjective that is correct in each sentence.

1. My grade on this test was (bad, worse) than my grade on the last one.

2. Is your sister a (good, better) cook?

3. Ron is the (better, best) writer in the class.

4. Dixie has decided to eat (less, least) sweets.

5. Joe earned his (good, best) score in today's meet.

6. Sean is a (better, best) goalie than Frank.

7. Aaron has collected (many, most) stamps.

8. The Drama Club has (more, most) members than the Fitness Club.

9. Mia's project is the (better, best) one in the Science Fair.

10. I just gave the (worse, worst) speech of my life!

UNIT TEST

Part 1
Matching Definitions

Match each word in Column A with its definition in Column B.

Column A	Column B
_____ **1.** Adjective	**A.** adjective that comes after the noun or pronoun it describes
_____ **2.** Comparative form	**B.** form of an adjective used to compare two people or things
_____ **3.** Definite article	**C.** word that describes or tells about a noun or pronoun
_____ **4.** Indefinite article	**D.** adjective form of a proper noun
_____ **5.** Proper adjective	**E.** form used to describe more than two people or things
_____ **6.** Predicate adjective	**F.** *the;* used to talk about a particular person, place, thing, or idea
_____ **7.** Superlative form	**G.** *a* and *an;* used to talk about a general group of people, places, things, or ideas

Part 2
Identifying Adjectives

Underline the adjective in the sentence. Write the noun or pronoun it describes on the line.

1. Clare wore a blue dress to the dance. _____

2. My father planted three trees in the yard. _____

3. Did you see my green sweater? _____

4. The noisy student bothered her classmates. _____

5. A spotted frog jumped from the garden. _____

Part 3
Identifying Articles

Underline the article that correctly completes each sentence.

1. Ryan and (the, a) baseball team won the state championship.

2. Will left home over (a, an) hour ago.

3. Rico is studying to be (a, an) architect.

4. Put (the, an) apples in my basket.

5. Adam bought (a, an) new pair of jeans.

Part 4
Proper Adjectives

Underline the proper adjective in the sentence. Write the noun it describes on the line.

1. Rita wants to sleep in an Irish castle. _____

2. Pat made Belgian waffles for breakfast. _____

3. I will meet you at the Mexican restaurant. _____

4. The sofa is made of Italian leather. _____

5. My report is on African wildlife. _____

Part 5
Nouns and Adjectives

Decide whether the word in bold is a noun or an adjective. Write *Noun* or *Adjective* on the line.

1. Dixie works at a **movie** theater. _____

2. The dance was held in the **gym**. _____

3. Barb enjoys reading **poetry**. _____

4. I will meet you at the **comedy** club. _____

5. What **movie** should we see? _____

Part 6
Comparisons

Underline the adjective that correctly completes each sentence.

1. Rick scored (fewer, less) points than Mark.

2. Alec is the (faster, fastest) runner on the team.

3. I hope to do (better, best) on this test than I did on my last test.

4. That was the (more, most) boring class I ever sat through!

5. Who is (younger, youngest)—Pete or Sam?

LESSON 24 # What Is an Action Verb?

KEY WORDS

Action verb
a word that tells what someone or something does, did, or will do

An **action verb** tells what the subject of a sentence does, did, or will do. Some verbs describe an action that you can see, such as *run* or *write*. Some verbs describe an action that you cannot see, such as *like* or *dream*.

Example Pat drives her sister to school every day.

Step 1: Who or what is the subject of the sentence?

Pat drives her sister to school every day. ◄— *Pat* is the subject.

Step 2: Find the word that tells what Pat is doing. Underline the verb.

Pat **drives** her sister to school every day. ◄— *Drives* is the verb.

A Underline the verb in each sentence.

1. Dan exercises every morning.

2. My family once lived on Maple Street.

3. The toddler ran to her mother.

4. Betty and Elle shopped at the mall.

5. We listened to George's new CD.

6. A bunny ran across the field.

7. The racecars zipped around the turn.

8. Will baked a yummy apple pie.

9. Mel's ice cream melted in the hot sun.

10. The alarm clock woke me up.

11. My family likes to ski.

12. Laura taped a poster in her locker.

13. My computer froze last night.

14. The noisy fans cheered for their team.

15. My friends always sit at the same lunch table.

A sentence can have more than one subject. It also can have more than one verb.

| Example | Al and Mark walked to the theater and saw a movie. |

Step 1: Who or what is doing something in this sentence?

Al and **Mark** walked to the theater ◄── *Al* and *Mark* are
and saw a movie.   the two subjects.

Step 2: Find the words that show what the subjects are doing. Underline the verbs.

Al and Mark <u>**walked**</u> to the theater ◄── *Walked* and *saw*
and <u>**saw**</u> a movie.   are the two verbs.

RULES TO REMEMBER

- An action verb tells what the subject does, did, or will do.

- Action verbs such as *walk* and *sit* describe something you can see.

- Action verbs such as *love* and *think* describe something you cannot see.

- A sentence can have more than one verb.

B **Underline the verbs in the sentences.**

1. Beth paid for her book and left the store.

2. Adam washed and waxed his car.

3. Sue opened the mailbox and took out the letter.

4. Mr. Daniels stopped and listened to Max.

5. The young child yelled and screamed for some candy.

6. Ben ate his sandwich and drank a carton of milk.

7. Rosa changed and went with her friends.

8. The police officer halted traffic and waited for the parade.

9. The audience watched the play and clapped for the actors.

10. I thought about the problem and chose an answer.

11. Mike wrote a poem and shared it with me.

12. Manny finished his homework and put his books away.

13. The frightened puppy barked and hid under the bed.

14. The football player jumped and caught the ball.

15. Chris drew a cartoon and sent it to the newspaper.

LESSON 25   What Is a State-of-Being Verb?

KEY WORDS

State-of-being verb
a verb that tells
something about the
condition of the subject
of a sentence; also
called a linking verb

A **state-of-being verb** explains or describes the subject of a sentence. The most commonly used state-of-being verb is *to be*. Other forms of this verb include *am, is, are, was, were, being,* and *been*. State-of-being verbs are also called linking verbs. Words like *sounds, appears, becomes, seems, turns, looks, tastes, smells,* and *stays* are state-of-being verbs.

Example   Tara is my best friend.

Step 1: Identify the subject of the sentence.

Tara is my best friend. ◄—— *Tara* is the subject.

Step 2: Find the state-of-being verb that links Tara to the description. Underline the verb.

Tara **is** my best friend. ◄—— *Is* is a state-of-being verb.

A   **Underline the state-of-being verb in each sentence.**

1. Maggie is at the skating rink every Monday.

2. Mrs. Hernandez looks tired today.

3. Todd is the captain of the football team.

4. This milk tastes sour.

5. Dan remained calm during the fire.

6. Jenna seems worried about something.

7. The band stayed on the field after the practice.

8. Emma was a member of the choir.

9. The boys are late for school.

10. That sweater looks great on you!

Many verbs can be either an action verb or a state-of-being verb. You can decide whether a verb shows action or a state of being. If the subject of the sentence is doing something, the verb is an action verb. If the subject is not doing something, the verb is a state-of-being verb.

Example   This pillow feels soft and fluffy.

Step 1: Identify the subject. Underline the verb that tells something about the subject.

This **pillow feels** soft and fluffy. ◄— *Pillow* is the subject; *feels* is the verb.

Step 2: Decide if the subject is doing something or not. Write *action* or *state-of-being* on the line

This pillow **feels** soft and fluffy. ◄— The pillow is not doing something; it is a state-of-being verb.

state-of-being

B Underline the verb in each sentence. Write *action* or *state-of-being* on the line to show how it is used.

1. The tiny bird grew stronger every day. _____

2. The farmers grew crops all year long. _____

3. Alison tasted her soup. _____

4. My soup tastes salty. _____

5. A rainbow suddenly appeared across the sky. _____

6. Matt appears worried about something. _____

7. Mica gets the Math award every year. _____

8. It gets dark earlier in January than in July. _____

9. Your ice cream sundae looks delicious. _____

10. Every evening, Nate looks at the stars through a telescope. _____

LESSON 26   Verb Tense

KEY WORDS

Tense
the time when an
action takes place

Simple tenses
the present, past, and
future forms of verbs

Perfect tenses
the present perfect,
past perfect, and future
perfect forms of a verb;
perfect tense describes
a completed action

A verb's **tense** shows when the action takes place. The three **simple tenses** are present, past, and future. The present tense shows the action is happening now. The past tense shows that the action has already happened. The future tense shows that the action will happen in the future.

Example   Kyle will sing at the dance.

Step 1: Identify the subject of the sentence. Underline the verb that tells what the subject is doing.

Kyle <u>will sing</u> at the dance. ◄—— *Kyle* is the subject.
Will sing is the verb.

Step 2: Think about when the action will happen. Write *present, past,* or *future* on the line to show the verb tense.

Kyle <u>will sing</u> at the dance. ◄—— The action will happen
future in the future.

A Underline the verb in the sentence. Write *present, past,* or *future* on the line to show the verb tense.

1. Ella talks on the phone for hours. _____

2. Walt jogged around the block. _____

3. Bill will drive me to school. _____

4. My sister cooked dinner. _____

5. The fans cheer for their team. _____

6. Who will win the game? _____

7. I send my brother e-mails. _____

8. Iman searched the Internet. _____

9. Rico reads two book a month. _____

10. We will clean the kitchen. _____

The **perfect tense** of a verb describes a completed action. The three perfect tenses are the present perfect, past perfect, and future perfect. The present perfect tense shows that the action took place in the past and continues to the present. The past perfect tense shows that one action was finished before another action started. The future perfect tense shows that an action will be completed before a certain time in the future.

Present Perfect	Past Perfect	Future Perfect
I have walked many miles.	I had walked many miles.	I will have walked many miles.
She has been a good student.	She had been a good student.	She will have been a good student.
We have ridden our bikes to school.	We had ridden our bikes to school.	We will have ridden our bikes to school.

Example   I had finished my homework before Matt arrived.

Step 1: Identify the action in this sentence. Underline the verb.

I **had finished** my homework before Matt arrived.

Step 2: Decide whether the verb tense is present perfect, past perfect, or future perfect. Write *present perfect, past perfect,* or *future perfect* on the line.

I **had finished** my homework before Matt arrived. The action was completed before another action started. The verb tense is past perfect.

past perfect

B Underline the verb in the sentence. Write *present perfect, past perfect,* or *future perfect* on the line to show its tense.

1. In May, we will have dated for one year. _____

2. The team has had a good season so far. _____

3. Marie had called Ted before the meeting. _____

4. The coach had reviewed the plays before the game. _____

5. After today, we will have studied for three days. _____

6. Barb has practiced her lines in the play. _____

7. My partner had started the lab before me. _____

8. Mike has traveled to Japan many times. _____

9. After Saturday, I will have dieted for one month. _____

10. Mr. Thomas has called my parents all week. _____

LESSON 27   Regular and Irregular Verbs

KEY WORDS

Regular verb
a verb whose past tense and past participle are formed by adding -d or -ed

Irregular verb
a verb whose past tense and past participle are formed in different ways

Regular verbs form their past tense and past participle by adding -d or -ed. **Irregular verbs** do not follow the usual rules. The past tense and past participle of an irregular verb take a different form. Below is a chart that shows some examples of regular and irregular verbs:

Regular and Irregular Verbs

	Present	**Past**	**Past Participle**
Regular Verbs	walk	walked	(had) walked
	dance	danced	(had) danced
	lift	lifted	(had) lifted
Irregular Verbs	ride	rode	(had) ridden
	begin	began	(had) begun
	see	saw	(had) seen
	break	broke	(had) broken
	fly	flew	(had) flown
	take	took	(had) taken
	choose	chose	(had) chosen

Example   Ricky goes to soccer practice.

Step 1: Identify the subject in the sentence.

Ricky goes to soccer practice. ◄— *Ricky* is the subject.

Step 2: Identify the verb in the sentence. Underline the verb.

Ricky **goes** to soccer practice. ◄— *Goes* is the verb.

Step 3: Ask yourself whether the past tense of this verb is formed by adding -d or -ed. If so, the verb is regular. If not, it is an irregular verb. Write *R* on the line if it is a regular verb. Write *I* on the line if it is an irregular verb.

Ricky **goes** to soccer practice. ◄— No. The past tense of *goes* is *went*. *Goes* is an **irregular** verb.

I

A **Underline the verb in each sentence. Write *R* on the line if it is a regular verb. Write *I* on the line if it is an irregular verb.**

1. I think about my science project. _____

2. I dig holes in the sand. _____

3. I walk every morning. _____

4. I lose my keys. _____

5. I catch fish in the lake. _____

6. I hear thunder in the distance. _____

7. I swing at the baseball. _____

8. I look out the window during class. _____

9. I lead the band onto the field._____

10. I bring lunch to school. _____

11. I bake good chocolate chip cookies. _____

12. I love my gift. _____

13. I eat tofu instead of meat. _____

14. I feed the dog twice a day._____

15. I hope that my dad wins a new car!_____

RULES TO REMEMBER

- Regular verbs form their past and past participle by adding *-d* or *-ed*.

- Irregular verbs do not follow the usual rules. The past tense and past participle of an irregular verb take a different form.

B More Practice. On the line, write the verb form that correctly completes each sentence. The present tense irregular verbs are shown in parentheses.

1. Emily _____ her math book home. (take)

2. I _____ Nate your e-mail address. (give)

3. A salesman _____ our doorbell. (ring)

4. Sue has _____ Todd for ten years. (know)

5. I _____ Larry at the party last night. (see)

6. Bill _____ Mia would call him. (know)

7. A tiny bird _____ through the open window. (fly)

8. Tony has already _____ a topic for his report. (choose)

9. My telephone has _____ a million times today! (ring)

10. Melanie _____ the Spanish test yesterday. (take)

11. The puppy _____ a bone under the tree. (hide)

12. The Clarks _____ from Philadelphia to Pittsburgh. (drive)

13. Paolo _____ to do his homework yesterday. (forget)

14. Coach Scott has _____ me some books on wrestling. (give)

15. Beth has _____ that dress to other dances. (wear)

LESSON 28   Subject-Verb Agreement

A verb must agree in number with its subject. When the subject is singular, add -s or -es to the present tense of the verb. When the subject is plural, use the plural form of the verb. The singular pronouns *I* and *you* are exceptions. They are singular subjects that use plural nouns. The chart below shows some combinations of subject-verb agreement:

Mary writes for the school paper.	Authors write books.	I write in my journal. Do you write poetry?
(singular subject/ singular verb form)	**(plural subject/ plural verb form)**	**(singular subject pronouns/plural verb forms)**

Example   Kelsey (enjoy, enjoys) dance class.

Step 1: Identify the subject of the sentence. Is the subject singular or plural?

Kelsey (enjoy, enjoys) dance class. ◄—— *Kelsey* is the subject. *Kelsey* is singular.

Step 2: Underline the verb that agrees with Kelsey.

Kelsey (enjoy, **enjoys**) dance class. ◄—— *Enjoys* is the singular verb form.

A Underline the verb in each sentence that agrees with the subject.

1. Chris (like, likes) to draw.

2. I (visit, visits) my grandparents every week.

3. Kyle and Shelly (write, writes) songs together.

4. Mrs. Diaz (decorate, decorates) her house for the holidays.

5. Stacy (watch, watches) the evening news.

6. My cousins (drive, drives) to Florida each spring.

7. Do you (work, works) at the pet shop?

8. Alex (play, plays) video games.

9. Ryan (jog, jogs) twice a week.

10. My parents (love, loves) our new car.

Most indefinite pronouns are singular even though their meanings are plural. They take the singular form of a verb. Some indefinite pronouns are always plural. They take the plural form of a verb. The chart below lists indefinite pronouns:

Singular			Plural
another	everybody	one	all
anybody	everyone	one another	both
any one	everything	somebody	few
anything	neither	someone	many
each	nobody	something	several
each other	no one		some
either	nothing		others

Example Everyone (is, are) excited about the concert.

Step 1: Decide if the subject of the sentence is singular or plural.

Everyone (is, are) excited about ◄—— *Everyone* is a singular the concert.   indefinite pronoun.

Step 2: Underline the verb that agrees with *everyone*.

Everyone (**is**, are) excited about ◄—— *Is* is the singular verb the concert.   form.

B Underline the verb in each sentence that agrees with the indefinite pronoun.

1. Several of the band members (go, goes) to Riverside High.

2. Everyone (is, are) welcome at the meeting.

3. Nothing (sound, sounds) as wonderful as the last period bell.

4. All of the players (work, works) hard in practice.

5. Many drivers (listen, listens) to the radio.

6. Few runners (finish, finishes) the marathon in under three hours.

7. One of the teachers (stay, stays) with the band.

8. All of the paintings (is, are) beautiful.

9. Does anybody (want, wants) another ice cream?

10. Something in the house (scare, scares) my puppy.

LESSON 29　Helping Verbs—To Do, To Be, To Have

KEY WORDS

Verb phrase
a main verb plus a
helping verb

Helping verb
a verb that combines
with a main verb to
show tense

Helping verbs combine with a main verb to show tense. Helping verbs include *be, am, is, are, was, were, been, being; has, have, had; do, does, did; can, will, shall, should, could, would, may, might, must.* The verbs *to do, to be,* and *to have* can be main verbs or helping verbs. A main verb plus a helping verb is called a **verb phrase**.

	Meaning as a main verb	**Meaning as a helping verb**
to do	to perform an action	helps form a question or verb phrase
	Paul did the laundry.	*Do you go to Seymour High?*
to be	to live or take a certain place	helps form a verb phrase
	My parents are at the play.	*They are writing a play.*
to have	to own or to possess	helps form the perfect tense
	Mark has his keys with him.	*Sal has begun her lesson.*

Example　Do you like strawberries?

Step 1: Find the verbs in the sentence. Do the verbs show action or state of being?

Do you **like** strawberries? ◄— *Do* and *like* are verbs. They show state of being.

Step 2: Decide if *do* is a helping verb. Write *main verb* or *helping verb* on the line.

Do you like strawberries? ◄— *Do* is a helping verb. It helps form a question.

helping verb

A The boldface word in each sentence is a form of the verb *to do.* Write *main verb* on the line if *to do* is used as the main verb. Write *helping verb* on the line if it is used as a helping verb.

RULES TO REMEMBER

■ Helping verbs combine with main verbs to show tense.

■ The verbs *to do, to be,* and *to have* can be main or helping verbs.

■ The number of words in the verb phrase can tell if the verbs are helping or main verbs.

1. Rico **did** his project yesterday. _____

2. **Did** Mrs. Dixon grade the tests? _____

3. I **do** not remember your name. _____

4. **Does** everyone want a drink? _____

5. My family **does** housework together. _____

B More practice. The boldface word in each sentence is a form of the verb *to be.* Write *main verb* on the line if *to be* is used as the main verb. Write *helping verb* on the line if it is used as a helping verb.

1. The car **is** in the garage. _____

2. **Are** you going to the picnic? _____

3. He **was** talking on the phone. _____

4. **Is** Dave with you? _____

5. You **are** always late for practice. _____

C More practice. The boldface word in each sentence is a form of the verb *to have.* Write *main verb* on the line if *to have* is used as the main verb. Write *helping verb* on the line if it is used as a helping verb.

1. Mark **has** two sisters. _____

2. **Have** you called Zack? _____

3. Ellen **has** answered my question. _____

4. My brother **has** my backpack. _____

5. Brian and Joan **have** finished the lab. _____

UNIT TEST

Part 1
Matching Definitions

Match each word in Column A with its definition in Column B.

Column A

____ **1.** Action verb

____ **2.** Helping verb

____ **3.** Irregular verb

____ **4.** Verb phrase

____ **5.** Regular verb

____ **6.** State-of-being verb

____ **7.** Tense

Column B

A. verb whose past tense and past participle are formed by adding *-d* or *-ed*

B. main verb plus a helping verb

C. the time when an action takes place

D. verb whose past tense and past participle are formed in different ways

E. word that tells what someone or something does, did, or will do

F. verb that combines with a main verb to show tense

G. verb that tells something about the condition of the subject of a sentence; also called a linking verb

Part 2
Identifying Verbs

Underline the verbs in each sentence.

1. Hal opened the door and greeted Mrs. Wilson.

2. Valerie sent me an e-mail.

3. Flashes of lightning lit the night sky.

4. Nancy washed and ironed her shirts.

5. The bus suddenly stopped in the middle of the road.

Part 3
State-of-Being Verbs

Underline the state-of-being verb in each sentence.

1. Mrs. Clark seems happy today.

2. That apple pie smells delicious.

3. The twins are on the baseball team.

4. Peter is the director of our play.

5. Mr. Hall was once mayor of our town.

Part 4
Verb Tense

Underline the verb in each sentence. Write *present, past,* or *future* on the line to show the verb tense.

1. Sasha will visit her grandmother in July. _____

2. Ted camped at the lake last week. _____

3. Carla enjoys country music. _____

4. Vicky made a movie about our school. _____

5. Bob ate dinner before the game. _____

Part 5
Subject-Verb Agreement

Underline the verb that correctly completes each sentence.

1. All of the Drama Club members (is, are) in the show.

2. My sister (watch, watches) cartoons on Saturday mornings.

3. Everyone (is, are) in the gym.

4. Abby and Zack (enjoy, enjoys) their art class.

5. Most of my friends (live, lives) in Oakdale.

Part 6
Helping Verbs

Decide if the boldface word in each sentence is used as the main verb or as a helping verb. Write *main* or *helping* on the line.

1. **Did** Eileen find her car keys? _____

2. Seth **had** finished the lab before I arrived. _____

3. Your backpack **was** near the door. _____

4. Lynn **is** trying on a new jacket. _____

5. Tom **was** waiting for me at the mall. _____

LESSON 30   What Is an Adverb?

KEY WORDS

Adverb
a word that describes a verb, an adjective, or another adverb

An **adverb** is a word that describes a verb, an adjective, or another adverb in a sentence. Many adverbs tell about action verbs. They describe *how, when,* or *where* the action happened. Adverbs that describe the way an action happened answer the question *how.* Adverbs that describe time answer the questions *when, how long,* and *how many times.* Adverbs that describe location answer the questions *where* or *in what direction.*

Example   Belle walked quickly down the street.

Step 1: Identify the verb in the sentence. The verb shows action.

Belle **walked** quickly down the street. ◄— *Walked* is the verb.

Step 2: Identify the adverb that describes the verb. Underline the adverb.

Belle walked **quickly** down the street. ◄— *Quickly* is the adverb.

Step 3: Decide if the adverb describes *how, when,* or *where* Belle walked. Write the question the adverb answers on the line.

Belle walked <u>quickly</u> down the street. ◄— The adverb *quickly* describes how Belle walked.

<u>how</u>

A The adverbs are underlined in the sentences below. Write *how, when,* or *where* on the line to show what question the adverb answers about the verb.

1. Rita <u>once</u> dated Joe. _____

2. Sam left his backpack <u>outside</u>. _____

3. Chew your food <u>slowly</u>! _____

4. The baby is resting <u>upstairs</u>. _____

5. Zack and I <u>often</u> study <u>together</u>. _____

6. The new driver <u>clumsily</u> parked his car. _____

7. Your flight will leave <u>shortly</u>. _____

8. Ethan <u>carefully</u> measured the room. _____

9. Lightning <u>suddenly</u> lit up the sky. _____

10. Chris plays the flute <u>well</u>. _____

11. Max called <u>twice</u> last night. _____

12. Mr. Tailor is waiting <u>inside</u> for you. _____

13. Meg <u>already</u> walked the dog. _____

14. The model walked <u>gracefully</u> across the stage. _____

15. Put your coat <u>here</u>. _____

B **More practice. Complete each sentence by writing an adverb that answers the question in parentheses.**

1. The car moved (how?) _____

2. Dad will be home (when?) _____

3. Put your books (where?) _____

4. Last week, Iman worked out (how many times?) _____

5. The fans cheered (how?) _____ for the team.

6. Your package will arrive (when?) _____

7. Jon has seen that movie (how many times?) _____

8. Turn (in what direction?) _____ at the corner.

9. Beth spoke (how?) _____ to her classmates.

10. I left my coat (where?) _____

11. Anna went to the mall (when?) _____

12. Seth read the directions (how?) _____

13. Pat visited her grandmother (how many times?) _____ this week.

14. Nate plays soccer (how?) _____

15. My puppy is hiding (where?) _____

LESSON 31   Recognizing Adverbs

KEY WORDS

Adverb
a word that describes a verb, an adjective, or another adverb

Adjective
a word that describes or tells about a noun or pronoun

Some words may be used as either **adverbs** or **adjectives**. The difference is in the way they are used in a sentence.

Example   Ryan pitched the last game.

Ryan pitched last.

Step 1: Look at the word *last* in the first sentence. What word in the sentence does *last* describe?

Ryan pitched the last **game**. ◄——— *Last* describes *game*.

Step 2: Decide what kind of word *game* is. Write *adverb* or *adjective* on the line.

Ryan pitched the last game. ◄——— *Game* is a noun.
                                  Last is an adjective.

<u>adjective</u>

Step 3: Look at the word *last* in the second sentence. What word in the sentence does *last* describe?

Ryan **pitched** last. ◄——————— *Last* describes *pitched*.

Step 4: Decide what kind of word *pitched* is. Write *adverb* or *adjective* on the line.

Ryan pitched last. ◄——————— *Pitched* is a verb.
                                  Last is an adverb.

<u>adverb</u>

A Decide whether the word in bold is an *adjective* or an *adverb*. Write your answer on the line.

1. Sue bought her **first** car. _____

2. Mia laughed **loudly** at the movie. _____

3. Ted entered the house **last.** _____

4. The audience clapped **loudly** for the actor. _____

5. Tony is a **fast** runner. _____

6. Don walked **carefully** along the icy path. _____

7. Marie writes a **daily** weather report. _____

8. Ella calls her mother **daily.** _____

9. Joe stood on **third** base. _____

10. Bo finished the race **third.** _____

Many adjectives can be changed into adverbs by adding the ending *-ly.* Adjectives that end in *y* are treated differently. Change the *y* to an *i* and add *-ly.*

| **Example** | In this sentence, the adjective can be changed to an adverb. |

Ed is a quick worker.

Step 1: Identify the word that describes a noun or pronoun. Underline the adjective.

Ed is a **quick** worker.

Step 2: Add the ending *-ly* to form an adverb from the adjective *quick.*

quick + ly   **quickly**

B Below are 10 adjectives. Change each adjective into an adverb. Write the adverb on the line.

1. late   _____

2. careful   _____

3. calm   _____

4. beautiful   _____

5. quick   _____

6. excited   _____

7. sad   _____

8. dangerous   _____

9. safe   _____

10. loud   _____

LESSON 32 Making Comparisons with Adverbs

KEY WORDS

Comparative form
the form of an adverb
that compares two
people or things

Superlative form
the form of an adverb
that compares more
than two people or
things

Adverbs are used to make comparisons. The **comparative form** is used to compare two people or things. The **superlative form** is used to compare more than two people or things. Follow these rules when forming the comparative and superlative forms.

Rule 1: Most one-syllable adverbs form the comparative and superlative forms by adding -er and -est. (quick, quicker, quickest)

Rule 2: Most adverbs with more than one syllable use more or most and less and least to form the comparative and superlative forms. (often, more often, most often)

Rule 3: A few adverbs are irregular. (well, better, best)

| **Example** | What are the comparative and superlative forms of *soon* and *costly?* |

Step 1: Look at how many syllables *soon* has. Review the rules above.

soon = **one syllable**

Step 2: Follow Rule 1 above for one-syllable adverbs.

soon + *er* = sooner ←——————— Comparative form

soon + *est* = soonest ←————— Superlative form

Step 3: Look at how many syllables *costly* has. Review the rules above.

cost + *ly* = **two syllables**

Step 4: Follow Rule 2 for adverbs with more than one syllable.

more + *costly* = more costly ←——— Comparative form

most + *costly* = most costly ←——— Superlative form

A Complete the chart to show the comparative and superlative forms of each adverb.

Adverb	Comparative Form	Superlative Form
softly		
well		
hard		
quickly		
late		
clearly		
slow		
often		

B Underline the form of the adverb that correctly completes the sentence. Then write *comparative* or *superlative* on the line.

1. Rose drove (more, most) slowly than Tim. _____

2. Pete is the (faster, fastest) runner on the team. _____

3. Sara sings (better, best) in front of an audience. _____

4. This is the (less, least) costly bracelet in the store. _____

5. Beth reads (more, most) often than Ella. _____

6. My diamond sparkles (less, least) brightly indoors than outdoors. _____

7. I like pizza (better, best) than tacos. _____

8. Do you know the (later, latest) score of the game? _____

9. Ryan pitches (better, best) on warm afternoons. _____

10. Which part of the test did you complete (more, most) quickly? _____

UNIT TEST

Part 1
Matching Definitions

Match each word in Column A with its definition in Column B.

Column A	Column B
____ **1.** Adverb	**A.** form of an adverb that compares more than two people or things
____ **2.** Adjective	**B.** form of an adverb that compares two people or things
____ **3.** Comparative form	**C.** word that describes or tells about a noun or pronoun
____ **4.** Superlative form	**D.** word that describes a verb, an adjective, or another adverb

Part 2
Identifying Adverbs

Underline the adverbs in each sentence.

1. My father will be home tomorrow.

2. I often stop here for gas.

3. Beth solved a very difficult problem.

4. Sue left her umbrella outside.

5. Lance ran quickly down the field.

6. Al seems quite worried lately.

7. Dr. Baker will be with you shortly.

8. The car slowly turned left at the traffic light.

9. Jon carefully dialed the telephone number.

10. Liang bought a very expensive bracelet.

Part 3
Adjectives and Adverbs

Decide whether the word in bold is an adjective or an adverb. Write *adjective* or *adverb* on the line.

1. Ella finished **first** in the spelling bee. _____

2. Eric is **usually** late for band practice. _____

3. Juan checks his phone messages **daily.** _____

4. You could hear a pin drop in the **quiet** room. _____

5. Mica had **hardly** begun his speech when the alarm went off. _____

6. Ted was **quite** pleased with his grade on the test. _____

7. The school nurse must finish her **daily** report. _____

8. Jack ate his **usual** breakfast of eggs and toast. _____

9. Did you think the test was **hard**? _____

10. My mother saved my **first** pair of shoes. _____

Part 4
Making Comparisons

Underline the form of the adverb that correctly completes each sentence. Then write *comparative* or *superlative* on the line.

1. Barb cheers (more, most) loudly than Eva. _____

2. This is the (more, most) boring book I ever read. _____

3. Tom is the (less, least) cheerful person I know. _____

4. Van's project is (less, least) complete than mine. _____

5. Bud is the (faster, fastest) runner on the track team. _____

6. Don speaks (more, most) clearly since his braces were removed. _____

7. Chris dates (less, least) often than Sheldon. _____

8. Kyle worked (harder, hardest) on his third research paper. _____

9. Dana began to speak (more, most) softly when Mr. Hall entered the room. _____

10. Jill is absent (less, least) often of them all. _____

LESSON 33 Prepositions and Prepositional Phrases

KEY WORDS

Preposition
a word that links a noun or pronoun and other words in a sentence

Prepositional phrase
a group of words that begins with a preposition and ends with a noun or pronoun

A **preposition** links a noun or pronoun and other words in a sentence. Each preposition has a specific meaning. A preposition is always a part of a **prepositional phrase**. Prepositional phrases begin with a preposition and end with a noun or pronoun. The chart below shows some commonly-used prepositions:

Prepositions

about	around	beneath	for	near	out	to
above	at	beside	from	of	over	under
across	before	down	in	off	past	until
after	behind	during	into	on	through	with

Example   The ice cream dripped on the floor.

Step 1: Look at the chart above. Underline the preposition in this sentence.

The ice cream dripped <u>on</u> the floor. ◄— *On* is the preposition.

Step 2: Identify the noun or pronoun that follows the preposition. Underline the noun.

The ice cream dripped <u>on</u> the **<u>floor</u>**. ◄— *Floor* is the noun.

Step 3: Underline the prepositional phrase.

The ice cream dripped <u>**on the floor**</u>.◄— *On the floor* is the prepositional phrase. It tells where the ice cream dripped.

A Underline the prepositional phrase in each sentence. Then write the preposition on the line.

1. The ball rolled down the hill._____

2. My brother is sitting near the stage. _____

3. Will opened a letter from Julie. _____

4. Diane left school without her books. _____

5. The frightened kitten hid beneath the bed. _____

6. School is closed for spring break. _____

7. Misha worked until midnight. _____

8. Jon lives by the park. _____

9. Nancy sat between her parents. _____

10. Everyone at the center took the test. _____

B More practice. Use each of these prepositional phrases in a complete sentence. Write each sentence on the line.

1. into the woods

_____

2. across the sky

_____

3. after the storm

_____

4. under the bridge

_____

5. for the party

_____

6. near the lake

_____

7. over the fence

_____

8. at the mall

_____

9. on her birthday

_____

10. through my window

_____

LESSON 34   Object of a Preposition

KEY WORDS

Object of a preposition
the noun or pronoun in a prepositional phrase

The **object of a preposition** is the noun or pronoun in a prepositional phrase. The object of a preposition may have adjectives in front of it.

Example   We walked along the icy path.

Step 1: Underline the prepositional phrase.

We walked **along the icy path**.

Step 2: Identify the noun or pronoun in the prepositional phrase. Write *noun* or *pronoun* on the line.

We walked <u>along the icy **path**</u>.   **noun**

A   Underline the object of the preposition in each sentence. Show what type of word it is by writing *noun* or *pronoun* on the line.

1. I gave the sweater to her._____

2. Josie stood between the coaches._____

3. Dave looked at my photographs. _____

4. Mac jogged around the corner. _____

5. Put your shoes beneath the bed. _____

6. Would you like a piece of the pie? _____

7. Rico left practice without me. _____

8. Take your paper off my desk._____

9. Anna studied until noon. _____

10. You must hit the ball within the lines. _____

The object of a preposition can be the objective form of a pronoun. Pronouns used as objects are *me, us, you, him, her, it,* and *them.* Usually, when the object is a pronoun, the phrase has only two words—the preposition and its object.

| **Example** | Tia tried not to laugh at (they, them).

At is the preposition. The objective form of the pronoun is *them*. Underline the correct object of the preposition *at*.

Tia tried not to laugh at (they, **them**).

B Underline the pronoun that correctly completes each sentence.

1. Julie went to the dance with (I, me).

2. Ted bought lunch for (us, we).

3. Did you study with (he, him)?

4. Wes took the money from (me, mine).

5. The test tube has a crack in (its, it).

6. My mother baked a cake for (yours, you).

7. I will speak after (he, him).

8. Did you send an e-mail to (her, she)?

9. A bee is buzzing around (us, we).

10. Did Mr. King leave before (they, them)?

C More practice. Underline the prepositional phrases in each sentence. Write the objects on the line.

1. Carl zoomed down the icy hill on his sled. _____

2. We walked through the door of the empty house. _____

3. Jed sat on the bench between Carol and me. _____

4. After the play, Marie went home with Angela. _____

5. Iman bought a dress for the dance at the mall. _____

6. Before school, Tom ate breakfast with her. _____

7. Max put his uniform on a hanger in his locker. _____

8. The ball rolled under the car on the driveway. _____

9. During the game, the fans clapped for the team. _____

10. Sal looked at my collection of postcards. _____

LESSON 35 Adjective and Adverb Phrases

KEY WORDS

Adjective phrase
a prepositional phrase that describes *which one, what kind,* or *how many* about a noun in a sentence

Adverb phrase
a prepositional phrase that describes *how, when, where, how much,* or *how long* about a verb, adjective, or another adverb in a sentence

You can use a prepositional phrase as an **adjective phrase**. An adjective phrase describes *which one, what kind,* or *how many* about a noun in a sentence. An adjective phrase always follows the noun it describes. An adjective phrase can describe the object of another preposition.

Example Kyle read a book about football.

Step 1: Look for a prepositional phrase that is used as an adjective. Underline the phrase.

Kyle read a book **about football**.

Step 2: What noun does the adjective phrase describe? Write the noun on the line.

Kyle read a **book** about football.   **book**

A Underline the adjective phrase in each sentence. Write the noun it describes on the line.

1. Kim bought a ticket to the show. _____

2. Do you have money for lunch? _____

3. The man behind Alice is my uncle. _____

4. The family on the fourth floor has a cat. _____

5. Tony wore a blue sweater with white trim. _____

6. The dress in the store window is beautiful. _____

7. A couple from Oakdale High won the dance contest. _____

8. Ellen wrote a report about the Civil War. _____

9. My favorite shop at the mall is closed. _____

10. All of my classmates passed the test. _____

You can use a prepositional phrase as an **adverb phrase**. An adverb phrase describes a verb, adjective, or another adverb in a sentence. An adverb phrase describes *how, when, where, how much,* or *how long.*

Example   Ed and Barb studied for two hours.

Step 1: Look for the prepositional phrase that is used as an adverb. Underline the phrase.

Ed and Barb studied **<u>for two hours</u>**.

Step 2: What word does the adverb phrase describe? Write the word on the line.

Ed and Barb **studied** <u>for two hours</u>.   <u>studied</u>

B Underline the adverb phrase in each sentence. Write the verb it describes on the line.

1. Sean threw the ball over the house. _____

2. Jason slept during the assembly. _____

3. Chris often exercises in the gym. _____

4. School was closed during the snowstorm. _____

5. Put your coat in your locker. _____

6. The ballerina danced across the stage. _____

7. Sue put her cell phone in her backpack. _____

8. My family will spend two weeks at the beach. _____

9. Your clothes will be ready on Friday. _____

10. Claire leaves for college today. _____

UNIT TEST

Part 1
Matching Definitions

Match each word in Column A with its definition in Column B.

Column A   **Column B**

____ **1.** Adjective phrase   **A.** group of words that begins with a preposition and ends with a noun or pronoun

____ **2.** Adverb phrase   **B.** word that links a noun or pronoun and other words in a sentence

____ **3.** Object of a preposition   **C.** describes *which one, what kind,* or *how many* about a noun

____ **4.** Preposition   **D.** noun or pronoun in a prepositional phrase

____ **5.** Prepositional phrase   **E.** describes *how, when, where, how much,* or *how long* about a verb

Part 2
Prepositions and
Prepositional Phrases

Underline the prepositional phrase in each sentence. Then write the preposition on the line.

1. The ball rolled under my neighbor's car. _____

2. Joan slept until noon. _____

3. We shoveled the driveway after the snowstorm. _____

4. My family is moving to Florida. _____

5. Jack starts his new job in one week. _____

6. Our seats are near the stage. _____

7. Did you get a letter from Dave? _____

8. A tiny bunny scampered into the woods. _____

9. The baby crawled toward her mother. _____

10. I will meet you at the bowling alley. _____

Part 3
Objects of Prepositions

Underline the prepositional phrase in each sentence. Then write the object of the preposition on the line.

1. Nate spoke with the new soccer coach. _____

2. Is Anna sitting at your lunch table? _____

3. Sara jogged around the track. _____

4. Jack bought flowers for Meg. _____

5. I lost Ron in the crowd. _____

6. Ryan hit the baseball over the fence. _____

7. Strong winds blew a shutter off the house. _____

8. Jack fell asleep during the movie. _____

9. Eva always exercises before work. _____

10. I must be home by midnight. _____

Part 4
Adjective Phrases and Adverb Phrases

Underline the prepositional phrase in each sentence. Write whether it is an *adjective phrase* or an *adverb phrase* on the line.

1. Zack rode his bicycle to the game. _____

2. The mayor of our town is visiting Elmwood High School. _____

3. The girl in the red shirt is my sister. _____

4. Put your coat on the chair. _____

5. Mr. Peters bought a house by the lake. _____

6. Conor read a book about the Civil War. _____

7. Juan worked for six hours yesterday. _____

8. The band marched onto the field. _____

9. Russ brought a cake to the party. _____

10. Ben wrote a song about our school. _____

LESSON 36   Coordinating Conjunctions

KEY WORDS

Conjunction
a word that connects related words or groups of words

Coordinating conjunction
a conjunction that connects words or groups of words that do the same job in a sentence

A **conjunction** is a word that connects two or more parts of a sentence. If the parts have the same job, they are connected by a **coordinating conjunction**. Following is a list of coordinating conjunctions:

and   or   but   nor   for   so   yet

Example | The movie was long but interesting.

Step 1: Identify the two words that have the same job in the sentence. Underline the words.

The movie was **long** but **interesting**. ◄──── Both words describe *movie*.

Step 2: What coordinating conjunction connects the two words? Write the conjunction on the line.

The movie was <u>long</u> **but** <u>interesting</u>.◄──── *But* connects *long* and *interesting*.

but

A Write the coordinating conjunction on the line. Underline the words it connects in the sentence.

1. Rita and Beth take piano lessons. _____

2. Maury washed and waxed the floor. _____

3. Do you want a hamburger or a hot dog? _____

4. Walt enjoys tennis and golf._____

5. I gave the papers to Zack and Brian. _____

6. Did Carla or Meg call you? _____

7. My vacation was brief but restful._____

8. Dee will go to the dance with Ed or Marco. _____

9. I bought and wrapped a gift for Jack. _____

10. The children shouted "trick or treat!" _____

A coordinating conjunction can connect two or more sentences. Use a comma to separate sentences joined with *and, but, nor, or, for, so,* or *yet*. Place a comma where the period is. Replace the capital letter in the second sentence with a lowercase letter.

Example Mrs. Lind enjoys cooking. She dislikes gardening.

Step 1: Which coordinating conjunction would best connect the sentences?

Mrs. Lind enjoys cooking.   She dislikes gardening.

Since Mrs. Lind's feelings differ, use **but**.

Step 2: Add the coordinating conjunction. Place a comma before the coordinating conjunction. Lowercase the capital letter in the second sentence.

Mrs. Lind enjoys cooking, **but s**he dislikes gardening.

B Use a coordinating conjunction to combine each pair of sentences. Place a comma where needed. Write the new sentence on the line.

1. Hank finished his homework. His brother went to sleep.

_____

2. Ellen can set the table. Peter can wash the dishes.

_____

3. Tess looked out the window. She didn't see Sophie leave the room.

_____

4. Dave went to band practice. He could not play his flute.

_____

5. We can order a pizza. We can make sandwiches.

_____

LESSON 37   Subordinating Conjunctions

KEY WORDS

Independent clause
a group of words that
expresses a complete
thought

Dependent clause
a group of words that
does not express a
complete thought

**Subordinating
conjunction**
a conjunction that
connects a dependent
clause to an
independent clause

An **independent clause** is a group of words that expresses a complete thought. A **dependent clause** is a group of words that does not express a complete thought. **Subordinating conjunctions** join these two kinds of clauses. Common subordinating conjunctions include:

after	although	so	wherever
in order that	since	where	if
when	whenever	because	until
even though	as	unless	while

Example   The players sing the school song whenever the team wins.

Step 1: Identify the group of words that expresses a complete thought.

The players sing the school song whenever the team wins.

Step 2: Identify the group of words that does not express a complete thought. Underline the dependent clause.

The players sing the school song **whenever the team wins.**

Step 3: Identify the subordinating conjunction that joins the two clauses. Write the conjunction on the line.

The players sing the school song **whenever** the team wins.

whenever

A Underline the dependent clause in the sentence. Write the subordinating conjunction on the line.

1. Dan was late because his clock is broken. _____

2. I made dinner since my mother is ill. _____

3. My puppy chewed on the shoe until I stopped him. _____

4. Jon plays golf whenever he can. _____

5. You should study if you want to pass the test. _____

6. A rainbow crossed the sky after the storm ended. _____

7. Tess worked on her report until the bell rang. _____

8. Donna talked on the phone while she made dinner. _____

9. The picnic will start at noon unless it rains._____

10. I rarely go to the library although I like to read._____

Sometimes a sentence begins with a dependent clause. Put a comma at the end of the clause.

RULES TO REMEMBER	

■ An independent clause is a sentence that expresses a complete thought.

■ A dependent clause does not express a complete thought.

■ A dependent clause may be at the beginning or end of a sentence.

■ When a dependent clause begins the sentence, follow it with a comma.

Example Although I enjoy music I do not know how to play an instrument.

Step 1: Look for the dependent clause at the beginning of this sentence. Underline the clause.

<u>**Although I enjoy music**</u> I do not know how to play an instrument.

Step 2: Place a comma after the dependent clause.

<u>Although I enjoy music</u>, I do not know how to play an instrument.

Step 3: Find the subordinating conjunction that joins the dependent clause to the independent clause. Write the subordinating conjunction on the line.

<u>**Although**</u> <u>I enjoy music</u>, I do not know how to play an instrument.   Although

B **Underline the dependent clause in each sentence. Add a comma where it is needed. Write the subordinating conjunction on the line.**

1. Since it is Saturday I slept until noon. _____

2. Until the traffic clears I will stay at work. _____

3. While waiting for the doctor Rick read a magazine. _____

4. Even though she is afraid of heights my sister enjoyed her first airplane ride. _____

5. If you want to lose weight you should exercise daily. _____

6. As if by magic a twenty-dollar bill fell into my lap. _____

7. When Luke leaves the room we will talk about his surprise party._____

8. After school ended we drove to Tony's house. _____

9. Because she had a sore throat the singer cancelled her show._____

10. When the Colonel walked into the room the soldiers saluted._____

LESSON 38 Correlative Conjunctions

KEY WORDS

Correlative conjunctions
a pair of conjunctions that connects words or groups of words that are related

Compound subject
two or more subjects connected by a conjunction

Correlative conjunctions express a shared relationship. They are always used in pairs. This chart shows the most common pairs of correlative conjunctions:

| both.....and | neither.....nor | whether.....or |
| either.....or | not only.....but also | |

Example Neither Sam nor Sue knows how to drive a car.

Look for the words that connect two related words. Underline the correlative conjunctions.

Neither Sam **nor** Sue knows how to drive a car.   The correlative conjunctions connect *Sam* and *Sue*.

A Underline the correlative conjunctions in each sentence.

1. Whether Ali invites Dee or Barb, she will take someone to the concert.

2. Neither Frank nor Bob wrote this letter.

3. Not only did Carey win the race, but he also finished in record time.

4. Both the mayor and the governor visited our school.

5. Either Sue or Tom will drive you home.

6. Not only did Nancy cook dinner, but she also baked cake.

7. Whether the bell rings or not, school ends at 3:15 P.M.

8. Neither my mother nor my father helps me with my homework.

9. Either Rita or Eddie left this message.

10. Both Gail and Hank are in the school band.

Sometimes two or more singular subjects are joined by a conjunction. Then they form a **compound subject**. Use the plural verb form when two or more subjects are joined with *and*. Use the singular verb form when two singular subjects are joined with *or* or *nor*. The verb must agree with the subject nearest the verb when one singular subject and one plural subject is joined with *or* or *nor.*

Example   Neither Seth nor his parents (knows, know) my address.

Step 1: Look for the singular and plural subject. Identify the subject that is nearest the verb.

Neither Seth nor his **parents**   *Parents* is a plural subject.
(knows, know) my address.

Step 2: Underline the verb form that agrees with the plural subject.

Neither Seth nor his parents (knows, **know**) my address.

B **Underline the verb form that correctly completes the sentence.**

1. Both my friends and neighbors (is, are) helping me clean the park.

2. Neither Bud nor Anna (own, owns) a pet.

3. Either players or their coach (call, calls) the newspaper.

4. Neither Rosa nor her brothers (drive, drives) a van.

5. Either the actors or the director (speak, speaks) to the audience.

6. Not only Rico but also Jan (was, were) in the gym.

7. Both Mr. and Mrs. Lewis (is, are) on the committee.

8. Either my mother or my sisters (make, makes) breakfast.

9. Both Mark and Luanne (deliver, delivers) newspapers.

10. Either Janice or her cousins (collect, collects) stamps.

LESSON 39   Interjections

KEY WORDS

Interjection
a word or phrase that expresses a feeling and is not related to other parts of a sentence

An **interjection** is a word or phrase that expresses a feeling. Interjections are independent words or phrases. They are not related to other parts of the sentence. They are used at the beginning or end of sentences.

Example   Oh boy, are you in trouble!

Find the words that express a strong feeling. Underline the interjection.

Oh boy, are you in trouble!

A Underline the interjection in each sentence.

1. Ouch! My head is throbbing!

2. Can you put these books in my car, please?

3. Stop! Look both ways before crossing the street.

4. Thanks, I needed a hug.

5. Hey, don't drink my soda.

6. Wow! That dress looks great on you!

7. What? You did not finish your homework?

8. No kidding? Tom asked you to the prom?

9. Quiet! Everyone is studying.

10. Sorry. I forgot to mail your letter.

Punctuation separates an interjection from the rest of the sentence. The punctuation can be a period, a comma, a question mark, or an exclamation point. When you use end punctuation after an interjection, capitalize the first word that follows. If you use a comma, do not capitalize the next word.

Example   Ah now I know how to solve the problem.

Step 1: Identify the interjection. Then underline it.
<u>Ah</u> now I know how to solve the problem. ◄ *Ah* is the interjection.

Step 2: A period, a comma, a question mark, or an exclamation point could be used.

Ah**!** now I know how to solve the problem. ◄ *Ah* expresses surprise. Use an exclamation point.

Step 3: Capitalize the first word that follows the interjection.

Ah! **N**ow I know how to solve the problem.

B **Add punctuation to separate the interjection and the rest of the sentence. Underline any words that should be capitalized.**

1. so who wants to take a vacation

2. hurry the bus is coming down the street

3. stop don't say another word

4. so what who cares if it rains

5. yes i can work tonight

6. i lost your pen sorry

7. look out you almost stepped on the cat

8. hush the baby is sleeping

9. gosh i don't know what to say

10. ha that was a good joke

UNIT TEST

Part 1
Matching Definitions

Match each word in Column A with its definition in Column B.

Column A	Column B
_____ **1.** Compound subject	**A.** group of words that does not express a complete thought
_____ **2.** Conjunction	**B.** pair of conjunctions that connects words or groups of words that are related
_____ **3.** Coordinating conjunction	**C.** conjunction that connects words or groups of words that do the same job in a sentence
_____ **4.** Correlative conjunctions	**D.** conjunction that connects a dependent clause to an independent clause
_____ **5.** Dependent clause	**E.** two or more subjects connected by a conjunction
_____ **6.** Independent clause	**F.** word that connects related words or groups or words
_____ **7.** Interjection	**G.** group of words that expresses a complete thought
_____ **8.** Subordinating conjunction	**H.** word or phrase that expresses a feeling and is not related to other parts of a sentence

Part 2
Coordinating Conjunctions

Write the coordinating conjunction on the line. Underline the words it connects in the sentence.

1. Dan did not win the race, nor did Max. _____

2. Ted washed and waxed his car. _____

3. The fair was fun but tiring. _____

4. Did you call Eddie or Rose? _____

5. The chili was spicy yet delicious. _____

Part 3
Subordinating Conjunctions

Circle the subordinating conjunction in each sentence. Underline the dependent clause.

1. Tony read a magazine while he waited for the doctor.

2. After the storm ended, we walked along the beach.

3. I cannot leave my house until my sister calls.

4. My puppy follows me wherever I go.

5. Joe jumped out of bed when his alarm went off.

Part 4
Correlative Conjunctions

Underline the correlative conjunctions in each sentence.

1. Not only does Eva sing, but she also dances quite well.

2. Both Scott and Bud made the basketball team.

3. Either my mother or my father will call the principal.

4. Whether Pam passes or fails the test, she knows she tried her best.

5. Both Deb and Will called me last night.

Part 5
Interjections

Write each sentence on the line. Add punctuation where needed. Capitalize words as needed.

1. wow your new outfit looks great

   _____

2. oh no i left my homework in my bedroom

   _____

3. quiet the baby is sleeping

   _____

4. hurry you are going to miss the bus

   _____

5. ouch these new shoes hurt my feet

   _____

LESSON 40   Sentences with Direct Objects

KEY WORDS

Direct object
a noun or pronoun
that receives the
action of a verb

The action of a verb can be transferred to another person or thing in the sentence. The person or thing that receives the action is the **direct object.** The direct object is a noun or a pronoun. Direct objects answer the question *whom* or *what* after the verb. They are never part of a prepositional phrase.

Example   Alana kicked the ball into the net.

What is receiving the action of the verb?
Underline the direct object.

Alana kicked the **ball** into the net.

A   The verb in each sentence is in bold.
Underline the direct object in each sentence.

1. Kurt **put** the letter in his pocket.

2. Chris **drew** a cartoon for the school paper.

3. Mel **caught** two fish at the lake.

4. After the snowstorm, we **shoveled** the walkway.

5. **Did** you **walk** the dog?

6. Sasha **read** a book about Russia.

7. I **borrowed** a CD from Dawn.

8. Kim **sold** tickets to the fair.

9. Marva **packed** her clothes in a suitcase.

10. **Did** you **write** this poem?

A noun or a pronoun may be used as a direct object. When the direct object is a pronoun, it is in the objective form. Pronouns used as objects are: *me, us, you, him, her, it,* and *them.*

Example	Don drove Sue and (I, me) to school.

Underline the pronoun that is in the objective form.

Don drove Sue and (I, **me**) to school.

B **Underline the pronoun that correctly completes the sentence.**

1. Bud showed (we, us) his school ring.

2. Diane told (them, they) to stop talking.

3. Give (her, she) your jacket.

4. Coach Young told (we, us) about the game.

5. Did you see (he, him) at the mall?

C **More practice. Write the subject, verb, and direct object of each sentence on the lines.**

1. Frank put his keys on the table.

Subject _____ Verb _____ Direct Object _____

2. Did you eat the last piece of cake?

Subject _____ Verb _____ Direct Object _____

3. Barb finished her report in the library.

Subject _____ Verb _____ Direct Object _____

4. My neighbors are painting their fence.

Subject _____ Verb _____ Direct Object _____

5. I visited her after school.

Subject _____ Verb _____ Direct Object _____

LESSON 41   Sentences with Indirect Objects

KEY WORDS

Indirect object
a noun or pronoun that receives the direct object of an action verb

Some sentences have a direct object and an **indirect object.** The indirect object answers the question *to whom, to what, for whom,* or *for what* about the verb. It receives the direct object of the action verb. Indirect objects are never part of a prepositional phrase. They come after the verb and before the direct object.

Example   Angela wrote Evan a letter.

Step 1: Look for the action verb in the sentence. Underline the verb.

Angela **wrote** Evan a letter. ◄——— *Wrote* is the action verb.

Step 2: What did Angela write? Identify the direct object.

Angela <u>wrote</u> Evan a **letter.** ◄——— *Letter* is the direct object.

Step 3: Look for the word between the verb and before the direct object. It tells to whom Angela wrote. Write the indirect object on the line.

Angela <u>wrote</u> **Evan** a letter.   **Evan**

A Underline the verb in each sentence. Write the indirect object on the line.

1. Cara read her brother a story. _____

2. Ryan gave Barb his notebook. _____

3. The mayor offered Jack a job. _____

4. Mr. Diaz handed Mel an envelope. _____

5. Pedro found Alice a chair. _____

6. Marcus sent his sister a postcard. _____

7. Tia brought Adam his lunch. _____

8. Rhonda told Seth her e-mail address. _____

9. The electric company sent my family a bill. _____

10. Dan threw Chris the football _____

A noun or a pronoun may be used as an indirect object. When the indirect object is a pronoun, it is in the objective form. Pronouns used as objects are *me, us, you, him, her, it,* and *them.*

Example	Meg fixed (us, we) a snack.

Underline the pronoun that is in objective form.

Meg fixed (**us,** we) a snack.

B **Underline the pronoun that correctly completes the sentence.**

1. Shelly lent (she, her) some money.

2. Mrs. Liang taught (them, they) chess.

3. Pete made (I, me) breakfast.

4. Mrs. Fisher ordered (we, us) uniforms.

5. Maria sang (him, he) a song.

C **More practice. Write the subject, verb, direct object, and indirect object of the sentence on the lines.**

1. Would you give Pat this message?

Subject _____   Direct Object _____

Verb _____   Indirect Object _____

2. The new waitress served us lunch.

Subject _____   Direct Object _____

Verb _____   Indirect Object _____

3. Carol knitted Larry a scarf.

Subject _____   Direct Object _____

Verb _____   Indirect Object _____

4. Give you parents this letter.

Subject _____   Direct Object _____

Verb _____   Indirect Object _____

5. Did Marco show you his new car?

Subject _____   Direct Object _____

Verb _____   Indirect Object _____

LESSON 42 Sentences with Object Complements

KEY WORDS

Object complement
a noun or an adjective that follows and refers to the direct object

An **object complement** is a noun or an adjective that adds meaning to the direct object. The object complement comes after the direct object in a sentence. It either renames or describes the direct object. Sometimes a sentence has a compound verb. Each verb can have its own direct object. Each direct object can have its own object complement.

Example   We named our dog Mickey and our cat Donald.

Step 1: Look for the direct objects of this sentence.

We named our **dog** Mickey and   *Dog* and *cat*
our **cat** Donald.   are direct objects.

Step 2: Look for the words that rename or describe the direct objects. Underline the object complements.

We named our dog **Mickey** and our cat **Donald**.
Mickey renames *dog*. *Donald* renames *cat*.

A Underline the object complements in each sentence.

1. Rex finds Algebra difficult.

2. The principal declared Jodie "Student of the Month."

3. My teammates elected me captain.

4. Marcie dyed her hair blonde.

5. The long drive made the baby cranky.

6. I painted my toenails pink and my fingernails red.

7. The long hike left me exhausted.

8. We voted Mrs. Forman "Best Teacher."

9. Emma named her cat Whiskers.

10. The bumpy ride made me nervous.

A question or a command can have a direct object and an object complement.

Example | Serve the coffee hot.

Step 1: Look for the word that receives the action of the verb. Write the direct object on the line.

Serve the **coffee** hot.   *Coffee* is the direct object.

<u>coffee</u>

Step 2: Look for the word that describes the direct object *coffee*. Write the object complement on the line.

Serve the coffee **hot**.   *Hot* describes *coffee*.

<u>hot</u>

B Write the direct object and object complement of each sentence on the line.

1. Color the apple red.

Direct object _____   Object complement _____

2. Can you dye your shoes blue?

Direct object _____   Object complement _____

3. Would you elect Barb treasurer?

Direct object _____   Object complement _____

4. Make the icing yellow.

Direct object _____   Object complement _____

5. Did you name the puppy Rusty?

Direct object _____   Object complement _____

LESSON 43   Sentences with Subject Complements

KEY WORDS

Subject complement
a noun, pronoun, or adjective that comes after a linking verb and adds meaning to the subject of the sentence

Predicate noun
a noun or pronoun that follows a linking verb and renames the subject

Predicate adjective
an adjective that follows a linking verb and describes the subject

A **subject complement** is a word that adds meaning to the subject of a sentence. One type of subject complement is a predicate noun. A **predicate noun** is a noun or pronoun that follows a linking verb. It renames the subject of a sentence.

> **Example**   A bat is a mammal.
>
> **Step 1:** Look for the linking verb. Write the linking verb on the line.
>
> A bat **is** a mammal.   **is**
>
> **Step 2:** Look for the noun or pronoun that comes after the linking verb and renames the subject. Underline the predicate noun.
>
> A bat is a <u>mammal</u>.   *Mammal* renames *bat*.

A Underline the predicate noun in each sentence. Write the linking verb on the line.

1. Mr. Winters is a firefighter. _____

2. Tiger Woods is a professional golfer. _____

3. Mrs. Summers was once mayor of Oakdale. _____

4. The title of the book is Animal Farm. _____

5. The goalie will be Sara. _____

6. My brother was the winner of the race. _____

7. R.L. Stine is a popular author. _____

8. Rico is a great dancer. _____

9. Mr. Hall was principal of Wilson High. _____

10. My uncle is a smart businessman. _____

Another type of subject complement is a **predicate adjective.** A predicate adjective is an adjective that follows a linking verb. It describes the subject of a sentence. Linking verbs include *am, is, are, was, were, being,* and *been.* Words like *sounds, appears, becomes, seems, turns, looks, tastes, smells,* and *stays* are also linking verbs.

Example   This milk tastes sour.

Step: Look for the linking verb in the sentence. Write the linking verb on the line.

This milk **tastes** sour.   **tastes**

Step: Look for the adjective that comes after the linking verb and describes the subject. Underline the predicate adjective.

This milk tastes **sour.**   *Sour* describes *milk.*

B Underline the predicate adjective in each sentence. Write the linking verb on the line.

1. The weather will be stormy today. _____

2. This pillow feels lumpy. _____

3. Is the music too loud? _____

4. The edge of the knife is very sharp. _____

5. You look wonderful in that sweater! _____

6. Is the cracker too salty? _____

7. Our substitute teacher seems nervous. _____

8. My skin feels dry. _____

9. Everyone seemed bored at the meeting. _____

10. Your report was terrific! _____

UNIT TEST

Part 1
Matching Definitions

Match each word in Column A with its definition in Column B.

Column A	Column B
____ **1.** Direct object	**A.** noun or pronoun that follows a linking verb and renames the subject
____ **2.** Indirect object	**B.** noun or pronoun that receives the direct object of an action verb
____ **3.** Object complement	**C.** noun or pronoun that receives the action of a verb
____ **4.** Predicate adjective	**D.** noun, pronoun, or adjective that comes after a linking verb and adds meaning to the subject of a sentence
____ **5.** Predicate noun	**E.** noun or adjective that follows and refers to the direct object
____ **6.** Subject complement	**F.** adjective that follows a linking verb and describes the subject

Part 2
Direct Objects

Underline the direct object in each sentence.

1. Rose is saving her money for a new car.

2. Did you attend the concert?

3. Frank called me from the beach.

4. Ryan plays baseball every spring.

5. Chris took notes during the class.

6. Larry made breakfast for his family.

7. Give the coat to Sue.

8. Jack wrote a story about our class trip.

9. My dog hid his bone under my bed.

10. Do you have a note for the teacher?

Part 3
Indirect Objects

Underline the indirect object in each sentence.

1. Mrs. Diaz bought Pam a gift.

2. Give me your jacket.

3. Alex gave Ron my address.

4. Lisa wrote her sister a letter.

5. The clerk handed Max his package.

6. Emma sent Tim an e-mail.

7. Rico lent Sue his dictionary.

8. Don showed me his pictures.

9. Did you ask Nancy a question?

10. Coach Scott brought the team a snack.

Part 4
Object Complements

Underline the object complement in each sentence.

1. Dan painted his room blue.

2. The basketball team elected Zack captain.

3. Mr. Hall makes our class interesting.

4. My father calls me Junior.

5. This watch turned my wrist green.

6. Eating a balanced diet keeps the body healthy.

7. The medicine made Pete sleepy.

8. Ted named his puppy Spot.

9. We painted the door red.

10. The umpire called the runner safe.

Part 5
Subject Complements

Underline the subject complement in each sentence.

1. This watch was an expensive gift.

2. Jesse Owens was an Olympic gold medal winner.

3. Your puppy is quite frisky.

4. This apple pie tastes delicious.

5. Mr. Dixon is a professional dancer.

LESSON 44 Verbals: Infinitives and Infinitive Phrases

KEY WORDS

Verbal
a verb form used as a noun or adjective in a sentence

Infinitive
a verb form made up of *to* plus a verb

Infinitive phrase
an infinitive and any words that help complete its meaning

A **verbal** is a verb form that is used as another part of speech. One kind of verbal is an infinitive. An **infinitive** is a verb form made up of *to* plus a verb. It is usually used as a noun. It may be used as an adjective or an adverb. Infinitives are not part of the main verb of a sentence. An **infinitive phrase** is an infinitive plus any words that help complete its meaning.

Example My parents want to vacation in Florida.

Step 1: Look for the verb form that is made up of *to* plus a verb. Underline the infinitive.

My parents want **to vacation** in Florida.   *to* + verb = infinitive

Step 2: Decide if the infinitive is used as a noun, an adjective, or an adverb. Write the part of speech on the line.

My parents want <u>to vacation</u> in Florida.   Names a person, place, thing, or idea.

noun

A Underline the infinitive or infinitive phrase in each sentence. Write *noun, adjective,* or *adverb* to show how it is used.

1. Ron offered to wash my car. _____

2. Nancy eats vegetables to stay healthy. _____

3. Beth likes to read mysteries. _____

4. Jonah is trying to solve the problem. _____

5. The team is eager to start the game. _____

6. Meg hopes to find her keys. _____

7. Sue promised to stop talking. _____

8. Do you have time to type a letter? _____

9. Hank needs to think about the plan. _____

10. Beth agreed to watch the baby. _____

The word *to* always starts an infinitive. It also starts some prepositional phrases. An infinitive is *to* plus a verb. A prepositional phrase is *to* plus a noun or pronoun. There is often an adjective after the word *to* in a prepositional phrase.

| **Example** | Everyone went to the gym after school. |

Everyone went to exercise after school.

Step 1: Look at the first sentence. Is *to* followed by a verb or by a noun or pronoun? Write *prepositional phrase* or *infinitive* on the line.

Everyone went **to the gym** after school.◄— *Gym* is a noun.

prepositional phrase

Step 2: Look at the second sentence. Is *to* followed by a verb or by a noun or pronoun? Write *prepositional phrase* or *infinitive* on the line.

Everyone went **to exercise** after school.◄—*Exercise* is a verb.

infinitive

B Decide whether the words in bold are an infinitive or a prepositional phrase. Write *infinitive* or *prepositional phrase* on the line.

1. Will the baby come **to me**? _____

2. Sam agreed **to pay** for lunch. _____

3. Did you take Evan **to the doctor**? _____

4. Wendy has **to leave** school early. _____

5. Zack is studying **to be** a pilot. _____

6. Can you give me directions **to the park**? _____

7. Lynn carried my backpack **to the bus**. _____

8. James delivered a package **to my neighbor**. _____

9. Bryan likes **to swim** in the ocean. _____

10. Sally wants **to have** a party. _____

LESSON 45   Verbals: Gerunds and Gerund Phrases

KEY WORDS

Gerund
a verb form ending
in *-ing* that is used
as a noun

Gerund phrase
a gerund and any
words that help
complete its meaning

A verbal is a verb form that is used as another part of speech. One kind of verbal is a gerund. A **gerund** is a verb ending in *-ing* that is used as a noun. Gerunds can be subjects, direct object, predicate nouns, or objects of prepositions. A **gerund phrase** is a gerund plus any words related to the gerund.

Example	Rico enjoys living in California.

Step 1: Look for the verb form ending in *-ing* . Underline the gerund.

Rico enjoys **living** in California.

Step 2: Decide if the gerund is used as a direct object, predicate noun, subject, or object of a preposition. Write the part of speech on the line.

Rico enjoys <u>living</u> in California. ◄——— *Living* receives the action of the verb *enjoys*.

Rico enjoys **living** in California.   **direct object**

A Underline the gerund in each sentence. Decide what part of speech it is used as. Write *direct object, predicate noun, subject,* or *object of a preposition* on the line.

1. Exercising keeps the body fit. _____

2. Strong pitching will win the game. _____

3. Bud's favorite sport is wrestling. _____

4. My chore was setting the table. _____

5. I enjoy being your friend._____

6. Skiing is a cold weather activity. _____

7. Mark knows swimming burns calories. _____

8. Building a house takes time. _____

9. Tom dislikes speaking into a microphone._____

10. Carl's job is delivering newspapers. _____

The progressive form of a verb also ends in *-ing*. You can tell the difference between this verb and the gerund. The progressive form of a verb is part of a verb phrase. It follows a helping verb. A gerund is always used as a noun.

Example   Pete is learning Spanish.

Pete enjoys learning new things.

Step 1: Look at the first sentence. Does the word ending in *-ing* come after a helping verb? Write *verb phrase* or *gerund* on the line.

Pete **is learning** Spanish.◄—— *Learning* comes after the helping verb *is*. It is part of a verb phrase.

Pete is learning Spanish.   **verb phrase**

Step 2: Look at the second sentence. Does the word ending in *-ing* come after a helping verb? Write *verb phrase* or *gerund* on the line.

Pete **enjoys learning** new things.◄—There is no helping verb. *Learning* is used as a noun.

Pete enjoys learning new things.   **gerund**

B **Decide whether the word in bold is part of a verb phrase or a gerund. Write *verb phrase* or *gerund* on the line.**

1. The fans are **cheering** for the team. _____

2. Jack is **rehearsing** his lines. _____

3. **Riding** a bicycle without a helmet is dangerous._____

4. Ed practiced **throwing** the football to Chris. _____

5. Dave enjoys **listening** to country music._____

6. Jake and Tiko are **writing** a play._____

7. Liz will be **waiting** for you in the hallway._____

8. The phone was **ringing** as I entered the house._____

9. Zack's hobby is **collecting** stamps._____

10. The band is **raising** money for new uniforms. _____

LESSON 46   Verbals: Participles and Participle Phrases

KEY WORDS

Participle
a verb that is used
as an adjective

Participle phrase
a phrase that includes
the participle and words
and phrases related to it

A verbal is a verb form that is used as another part of speech. One kind of verbal is a participle. A **participle** is a verb form that is used as an adjective. Participles can describe nouns, pronouns, or other adjectives. A participle plus any words that complement or describe it form a **participle phrase.**

> **Example**   Tony bought a used car.
>
> **Step 1:** Look for the verb form that describes a noun in this sentence. Underline the participle.
>
> Tony bought a **used** car.
>
> **Step 2:** Look at the noun that *used* describes. Write the noun on the line.
>
> Tony bought a <u>used</u> **car.**   **car**

A **Underline the participle in each sentence. Write the noun it describes on the line.**

1. These baked apples taste delicious. _____

2. Kyle is my swimming coach. _____

3. Frozen branches broke from the trees. _____

4. I took the cans to the recycling center. _____

5. The decorated gym looks wonderful! _____

6. Here is my finished report._____

7. Falling raindrops landed on the car's windshield. _____

8. Your bicycle's worn tires are unsafe._____

9. The baby eats steamed carrots._____

10. George ordered fried chicken for dinner. _____

Participles are used as adjectives. Verbs show action. You can tell the difference between words used as participles and words used as verbs. Ask yourself if the word or group of words show action or if they describe another word. If they show action, they are part of a verb phrase. If they describe another word, they are a participle or part of a participle phrase.

Example   Secrets <u>kept inside</u> can cause stress.

The street <u>was covered</u> with trash.

Step 1: Look at the underlined words. Do they show action or describe another word?

Secrets **<u>kept inside</u>** can cause stress. ◄ *Kept inside* describes *secrets*.

The street **<u>was covered</u>** with trash. ◄ *Was covered* shows action.

Step 2: Decide whether the underlined words in each sentence are a verb or a participle. Write *verb* or *participle* on the line.

Secrets <u>kept inside</u> can cause stress.   **<u>Participle</u>**

The street <u>was covered</u> with trash.   **<u>Verb</u>**

B **Decide whether the word in bold is part of a participle or verb phrase. Write *participle* or *verb* on the line.**

1. The man **sitting** next to me is my uncle._____

2. Put the **completed** form on my desk. _____

3. Mrs. Wallace has **graded** the tests. _____

4. **Glistening** stars lit the night sky. _____

5. Rico is **planning** a surprise party. _____

6. Sal and Jed have **painted** the dog house. _____

7. Water leaked from the **broken** glass. _____

8. The divers discovered a **sunken** ship. _____

9. Have you **eaten** lunch yet? _____

10. This shelf was made from **recycled** wood. _____

LESSON 47   More Practice with Verbals

KEY WORDS

Verbal phrase
a verbal plus any words
that help complete
its meaning

Infinitive
a verb form made up
of *to* plus a verb that is
used as a noun, an
adjective, or an adverb

Gerund
a verb form that ends
in *-ing* and is used
as a noun

Participle
a verb form that is
used as an adjective

The three kinds of verbals are infinitives, gerunds, and participles. An **infinitive** is *to* plus a verb. A **gerund** is a verb ending in *-ing* that is used as a noun. A **participle** is a verb that is used as an adjective.

Example   Mrs. Andrews is the person to call.

Calling long distance can be expensive.

His calling card is purple.

Step 1: Look at the first sentence. What verb in this sentence is a verbal? Underline the verbal. Write the kind of verbal it is on the line.

Mrs. Andrews is the person <u>to call</u>. ◄ *to* + verb = <u>infinitive</u>

Step 2: Look at the second sentence. What verb in this sentence is a verbal? Underline the verbal. Write the kind of verbal it is on the line.

<u>Calling</u> long distance can be expensive. ◄———— Verb ending in *-ing* used as noun = <u>gerund</u>

Step 3: Look at the third sentence. What verb in this sentence is a verbal? Underline the verbal. Write the kind of verbal it is on the line.

His <u>calling</u> card is purple. ◄———— Verb used as an adjective = <u>participle</u>

A   **Underline the verbal in each sentence. Decide what kind of verbal it is. Write *infinitive*, *gerund*, or *participle* on the line.**

1. Ron's favorite sport is bowling. _____

2. We sat around the blazing campfire. _____

3. Steve has a throbbing headache. _____

4. I want to finish my report tonight. _____

5. This car is easy to drive. _____

6. Smoking harms the body. _____

7. The road was covered with broken glass. _____

8. Your whistling is annoying me. _____

9. Are you ready to leave? _____

10. Dan sat on the freshly painted bench. _____

A **verbal phrase** is made up of a verbal and words that complete its meaning. Three types of verbal phrases are infinitive phrases, gerund phrases, and participle phrases.

Example	Rosa hopes to lose ten pounds.

Step 1: Look for the verb form that is used as another part of speech.

Rosa hopes **to lose** ten pounds. ◄— *to* + verb = infinitive

Step 2: Identify the words that complete the verbal phrase. Underline the verbal phrase. Write *infinitive phrase, gerund phrase,* or *participle phrase* on the line.

Rosa hopes **to lose ten pounds.**   **infinitive phrase**

B Underline the verbal phrase in each sentence. Write *infinitive phrase, gerund phrase,* or *participle phrase* on the line.

1. Beth is thinking about taking an art class. _____

2. Jed is the person standing behind Al. _____

3. Deb is studying to be a nurse. _____

4. Ryan tried to hit a home run. _____

5. Pat opened the package addressed to the school. _____

6. Emma spent the day cleaning her room. _____

7. The principal decided to send the students home. _____

8. Mary read the letter written by her sister. _____

9. Bob offered to help me study for the test. _____

10. I went to the store to buy school supplies. _____

UNIT TEST

Part 1
Matching Definitions

Match each word in Column A with its definition in Column B.

Column A

____ **1.** Gerund

____ **2.** Gerund phrase

____ **3.** Infinitive

____ **4.** Infinitive phrase

____ **5.** Participle

____ **6.** Participle phrase

____ **7.** Verbal

____ **8.** Verbal phrase

Column B

A. a verbal plus any words that help complete its meaning

B. an infinitive plus any words that help complete its meaning

C. verb form that ends in *-ing* that is used as a noun

D. verb form used as a noun or an adjective in a sentence

E. verb that is used as an adjective

F. verb form made up of *to* plus a verb

G. a gerund and any words that help complete its meaning

H. a phrase that includes the participle and words and phrases related to it

Part 2
Infinitives

Decide whether the words in bold are an infinitive or a prepositional phrase. Write *infinitive* or *prepositional phrase* on the line.

1. Do you want me **to call** your brother?_____

2. Lisa went **to band practice**._____

3. I gave the letter **to Mrs. Wallace**. _____

4. My family is going **to visit** Dee next week._____

5. What do you want me **to carry**?_____

6. Meg wants **to lose** some weight. _____

7. Randy gave his money **to the teller**._____

8. Barb agreed **to watch** the baby. _____

Part 3
Gerunds

Decide whether the word in bold is part of a verb phrase or a gerund. Write *verb phrase* or *gerund* on the line.

1. Mark is **planning** a surprise party for Marie._____

2. **Hiking** is a hobby of mine. _____

3. Mrs. Dixon thought about **leaving** work early. _____

4. Rosa enjoys **swimming** in the ocean. _____

5. Kyle is **saving** for college. _____

6. Dan is **studying** his notes. _____

7. The team is **listening** carefully to Coach Scott. _____

8. Anne finished **knitting** a sweater for Carl. _____

Part 4
Participles

Decide whether the word in bold is part of a participle or verb phrase. Write *participle* or *verb* on the line.

1. The baby likes **steamed** carrots. _____

2. A storm is **moving** toward our town. _____

3. I noticed the **crying** child. _____

4. Deb hung the **soaked** clothing on the line. _____

5. Sue has **dusted** the furniture. _____

6. Tom put a frame around the **finished** painting. _____

7. Do you know the woman **seated** on the bench? _____

8. The freshly **baked** pie smells wonderful. _____

Part 5
Kinds of Verbals

Underline the verbal in each sentence. Decide what kind of verbal it is. Write *infinitive, gerund,* or *participle* on the line.

1. Barb wants to go to the concert. _____

2. Skiing is Max's favorite sport. _____

3. Did you see a letter addressed to Tom? _____

4. The quilt covering the bed was beautiful. _____

5. Evan practiced solving word problems. _____

6. Scott likes to play tricks on his friends. _____

7. The children enjoy playing kickball. _____

8. Passing the test is my main goal. _____

LESSON 48   Phrases and Clauses

KEY WORDS

Phrase
a group of words
without a subject and a
predicate that relates to
part of a sentence

Clause
a group of words that
has a subject and a
predicate; a clause
may be independent
or dependent

Independent clause
a clause that expresses
a complete thought
and can stand alone
as a sentence

Dependent clause
a clause that does
not express a complete
thought and cannot
stand alone as
a sentence

Words can be organized into phrases and clauses. A **phrase** is group of words that work together. A phrase does not have both a subject and a predicate. A **clause** is a group of words with both a subject and a predicate. An **independent clause** expresses a complete thought and can stand alone as a sentence. A **dependent clause** does not express a complete thought and cannot stand alone as a sentence.

Example   After the snowstorm

Look for a subject and a predicate in the group of words.
Write *phrase* or *clause* on the line.

After the **snowstorm** ◄——— *Snowstorm* is a subject.

There is no predicate. The
group of words is a phrase.

After the snowstorm   **phrase**

A Identify whether each group of words is a phrase or a clause. Write *phrase* or *clause* on the line.

1. Because the car won't start _____

2. To enter the race _____

3. Near the post office_____

4. With my older sister _____

5. Since you are late _____

6. Running around the corner _____

7. Beth lives next door _____

8. For less than one hour _____

9. The baby cried all night _____

10. Which was in my locker _____

An independent clause expresses a complete thought and can stand alone as a sentence. A dependent clause does not express a complete thought. It cannot stand alone as a sentence.

Example   Until the bus arrives

Decide whether the clause expresses a complete thought. If so, it is an independent clause. If not, it is a dependent clause. Write *dependent* or *independent* on the line.

Until the bus arrives ◄——— This clause does not express a complete thought. The reader does not know what will happen until the bus arrives.

Until the bus arrives   **dependent**

B Decide whether each clause is dependent or independent. Write *dependent* or *independent* on the line.

1. When we reached the park _____

2. Since you are ill _____

3. Alex sings with the chorus _____

4. Your kitten tore my dress _____

5. Whoever said that _____

6. If you pass this test _____

7. That knocked on my door _____

8. He walked through the door _____

9. They left after lunch _____

10. Due to the fire _____

LESSON 49   Compound Sentences

KEY WORDS

Compound sentence
a sentence made up
of two independent
clauses that are
connected by a
conjunction

A **compound sentence** is a sentence with two related independent
clauses. Each clause has its own subject and verb. The clauses can be
connected by a coordinating conjunction. A comma usually comes
before the conjunction in a compound sentence.

Example   Jesse lost the race but he felt like a winner.

Step 1: Identify the independent clauses. Underline the clauses.

Jesse lost the race but **he felt like a winner.**

Step 2: Put a comma before the conjunction that connects the
independent clauses.

Jesse lost the race, but he felt like a winner.

A Underline the two independent clauses in each compound
sentence. Put a comma before the conjunction.

1. The campers can eat a late lunch or they can have an early dinner.

2. Mrs. Nelson bought some fabric and she made new curtains.

3. The picnic is cancelled for it has started to rain.

4. Judy needs a suitcase so she went to the mall.

5. Kim can buy a new dress or she can borrow one from me.

6. The party is cancelled for the guest of honor is sick.

7. Val dusted the furniture and she waxed the floor.

8. Rob called Bev and he asked her to the dance.

9. Mark woke up late so he missed the bus.

10. You can have a part in the play or you can help the stage crew.

Sometimes a semicolon is used between two closely related independent clauses instead of a comma and a conjunction.

Example	Dina does not get enough sleep, so she is always tired.

Step 1: Identify the conjunction that joins these two clauses. Cross out the conjunction.

Dina does not get enough sleep, ~~so~~ she is always tired.

Step 2: Replace the comma with a semicolon.

Dina does not get enough sleep; she is always tired.

B Cross out the conjunction joining the clauses in each sentence. Replace the comma with a semicolon.

1. Pat and Juan did not go to the movies, but they went bowling.

2. Jerry is a good driver, and he always wears his seatbelt.

3. You had better get to sleep, or you will be tired tomorrow.

4. Emma's bicycle is broken, so she had to walk to practice.

5. Larry did not buy my car, but he bought a motorcycle.

6. Bill stopped working out, so he has gained weight.

7. Sue should study her notes, or she might forget her speech.

8. You have worked hard, so there is no homework tonight.

9. Lynn is shy around strangers, yet she has a part in the play.

10. Chris enjoys baseball, but he likes football more.

LESSON 50   Kins of Dependent Clauses

KEY WORDS

Adverb clause
a dependent clause that tells something about a verb, an adjective, or another adverb

Noun clause
a dependent clause that works like a noun in a sentence

Adjective clause
a dependent clause that describes a noun or pronoun

A dependent clause does not express a complete idea and cannot stand alone as a sentence. An **adverb clause** is a dependent clause. It tells something about a verb, an adjective, or another adverb in a sentence. An adverb clause has a subject and a verb. It answers the questions *where, when, why, how much, how often,* and *how soon.*

Example   Marni joined the chorus because she likes to sing.

Look for the group of words that describes a verb, adjective, or adverb in this sentence. Underline the adverb clause.

Marni joined the chorus **because she likes to sing**.

This adverb clause answers the question

why Marni joined the chorus.

A   **Underline the adverb clause in each sentence.**

1. Marco finished his homework while he waited for the bus.

2. Before I met you, I never knew anyone with red hair.

3. Max stood up so that Mrs. Hale could sit down.

4. Until your car is fixed, I will drive you to work.

5. My cousin stays at my house whenever he has a day off.

A **noun clause** is a dependent clause. It works exactly like a noun in a sentence. A noun clause often begins with a relative pronoun. Relative pronouns are *who, whom, whose, which, that, what, whoever, whomever, whichever,* and *whatever.*

Example   Whoever needs a job should speak with Mr. Ruiz.

Look for the group of words that acts like a noun in this sentence. Underline the noun clause.

Whoever needs a job should speak with Mr. Ruiz.

This noun clause starts with the relative pronoun *whoever.*

B Underline the noun clause in each sentence.

1. Do you know what you want for lunch?

2. Ray hoped that his answer was correct.

3. Did you hear which team won the game?

4. Whoever owns that dog should buy a leash.

5. Please order whatever you want.

An **adjective clause** is a dependent clause. It describes a noun or a pronoun. An adjective clause usually follows the word it describes.

Example   My neighbor is the person who called the police.

Look for the group of words that describes a noun or pronoun. Underline the adjective clause.

My neighbor is the person **who called the police.**

This adjective clause describes *person*.

C Underline the adjective clause in each sentence.

1. The grand prize went to the student who sold the most magazines.

2. The college that Joe attends is in North Carolina.

3. Are you the person who called me last night?

4. Soccer is the sport that I like best.

5. The man who was in line ahead of me bought the last concert ticket.

LESSON 51   Complex Sentences

KEY WORDS

Complex sentence
a sentence with one
independent clause
and one or more
dependent clauses

A **complex sentence** has one independent clause and one or more dependent clauses. The dependent clause may be an adverb, noun, or adjective clause.

Example   The fans cheered loudly until the final buzzer sounded.

Look for the clause that expresses a complete thought and can stand alone as a sentence. Underline the independent clause.

The fans cheered loudly until the final buzzer sounded.

A Underline the independent clause in each sentence. A dependent clause may separate two parts of the independent clause.

1. The children played outside while their parents ate inside.

2. I will make dinner if you are too busy.

3. The man who sang The Star Spangled Banner is a policeman.

4. School was cancelled because the roads were icy.

5. I will buy this coat when it goes on sale.

6. The parade will begin at noon unless it starts raining.

7. You cannot play video games until your grades improve.

8. After the game ended, Marci gave the players cold drinks.

9. The gift that we gave Pat was expensive.

10. Ellen gave the man who found her cat a reward.

B **More practice. Add an independent clause to each dependent clause to form a complex sentence. Write the sentence on the line.**

1. that Ellie bought

_____

2. who is sitting in the front row

_____

3. because he overslept

_____

4. whoever owns that car

_____

5. whatever you want

_____

6. that is hanging in my locker

_____

7. if you try hard enough

_____

8. before school started

_____

9. where Joe works

_____

10. after the party ended

_____

UNIT TEST

Part 1
Matching Definitions

Match each word in Column A with its definition in Column B.

Column A   Column B

____ **1.** Adverb clause   **A.** group of words that has a subject and a predicate; may be dependent or independent

____ **2.** Adjective clause   **B.** dependent clause that describes a noun or pronoun

____ **3.** Clause   **C.** group of words without a subject and a predicate that relates to part of a sentence

____ **4.** Complex sentence   **D.** sentence with one independent clause and one or more dependent clauses

____ **5.** Compound sentence   **E.** dependent clause that works like a noun in a sentence

____ **6.** Noun clause   **F.** sentence made up of two independent clauses that are connected by a conjunction

____ **7.** Phrase   **G.** dependent clause that tells something about a verb, an adjective, or another adverb

____ **8.** Independent and clause   **H.** clause that expresses a complete thought can stand alone

____ **9.** Dependent clause   **I.** clause that does not express a complete thought and cannot stand alone

Part 2
Phrases and Clauses

Identify whether each group of words is a phrase or a clause. Write *phrase* or *clause* on the line.

1. After the snowstorm _____

2. Since she is taller _____

3. While you study your notes _____

4. Beneath a moonlit sky _____

5. Before the game begins _____

Part 3
Conjunctions

Cross out the conjunction joining the clauses in each sentence. Replace the comma with a semicolon.

1. Sue practiced her lines, yet she is nervous about performing in the play.

2. Dan overslept, so he missed the bus.

3. You did not stop at the light, and you are not wearing a seatbelt.

4. Ryan had better go to bed, or he will be tired tomorrow.

5. Meg enjoys jazz, but she likes country music more.

Part 4
Dependent Clauses

Underline the dependent clause in each sentence. Write whether it is an *adjective clause, adverb clause,* or *noun clause* on the line.

1. You can take whatever you want from the box. _____

2. Will left the theater before the play ended. _____

3. Beth met Pete, who is an old friend of mine. _____

4. Whoever wins the contest gets a gold medal. _____

5. The sweater that I made is quite comfortable. _____

Part 5
Independent Clauses

Underline the independent clause in each complex sentence. A dependent clause may separate two parts of the independent clause.

1. Max will give me a ride if I need one.

2. Since it is snowing, school is cancelled.

3. After the dance ended, we cleaned the gym.

4. Fans filed into the gym before the game began.

5. The poem that Wes wrote was dedicated to his parents.

GLOSSARY

Action verb a word that tells what someone or something does, did, or will do

Adjective a word that describes or tells about a noun or pronoun

Adjective clause a dependent clause that describes a noun or pronoun

Adjective phrase a prepositional phrase that describes which one, what kind, or how many about a noun in a sentence

Adverb a word that describes a verb, an adjective, or another adverb

Adverb clause a dependent clause that tells something about a verb, an adjective, or another adverb

Adverb phrase a prepositional phrase that describes how, when, where, how much, or how long about a verb, adjective, or another adverb in a sentence

Antecedent a noun that a pronoun replaces

Apostrophe a punctuation mark (') that shows a noun is possessive

Capital letter the uppercase form of a letter, such as A, B, C

Clause a group of words that has a subject and a predicate; a clause may be independent or dependent

Collective noun a word that names a group of people or things

Comma a punctuation mark (,) used to separate words or groups of words

Common noun the name of any person, place, thing, or idea

Comparative adjective an adjective that compares one noun with another

Comparative form the form of an adverb that compares two people or things

Complex sentence a sentence with one independent clause and one or more dependent clauses

Compound noun a noun that is more than one word

Compound relative pronoun a pronoun formed by combining a relative pronoun and *ever*

Compound sentence a sentence made up of two independent clauses that are connected by a conjunction

Compound subject two or more subjects connected by a conjunction

Conjunction a word that connects related words or groups of words

Consonant all the letters of the alphabet that are not vowels

Coordinating conjunction a conjunction that connects words or groups of words that do the same job in a sentence

Correlative conjunctions a pair of conjunctions that connects words or groups of words that are related

Declarative sentence a sentence that states a fact and ends with a period

Definite article the word *the*; it refers to a specific person, place, thing, or idea

Demonstrative pronoun a pronoun that points to nouns: *this, these, that,* and *those*

Dependent clause a group of words that does not express a complete thought

Direct object a noun or pronoun that receives the action of a verb

Direct quotation the exact words a person said

End punctuation a period (.), question mark (?), or exclamation point (!) that shows where a sentence ends

Exclamatory sentence a sentence that expresses strong feeling and ends with an exclamation point

First-person pronoun a pronoun that refers to the person who is speaking

Gerund a verb form ending in *-ing* that is used as a noun

Gerund phrase a gerund and any words that help complete its meaning

Helping verb a verb that combines with a main verb to show tense

Imperative sentence a sentence that gives a command and ends with a period

Indefinite article the words *a* and *an*; they refer to a general group of people, places, things, or ideas

Indefinite pronoun a pronoun that refers to a noun that is not named

Independent clause a clause that expresses a complete thought and can stand alone as a sentence

Indirect object a noun or pronoun that receives the direct object of an action verb

Indirect quotation a description of what a person said that is not the speaker's exact words; often introduced by the word *that*

Infinitive a verb form made up of *to* plus a verb

Infinitive phrase an infinitive and any words that help complete its meaning

Interjection a word or phrase that expresses a feeling and is not related to other parts of a sentence

Interrogative pronoun a word that introduces a question

Interrogative sentence a sentence that asks a question and ends with a question mark

GLOSSARY

Irregular verb a verb whose past tense and past participle are formed in different ways

Noun a word that names a person, place, thing, or idea

Noun clause a dependent clause that works like a noun in a sentence

Object complement a noun or an adjective that follows and refers to the direct object

Object of a preposition the noun or pronoun in a prepositional phrase

Participle a verb that is used as an adjective

Participle phrase a phrase that includes the participle and words and phrases related to it

Perfect tenses perfect tense describes a completed action; the present perfect, past perfect, and future perfect tenses of verbs

Personal pronoun a pronoun that refers to a person or thing

Phrase a group of words without a subject and a predicate that relates to part of a sentence

Plural noun the name of more than one person, place, thing, or idea

Positive adjective an adjective that describes one noun

Possessive noun a noun that shows ownership or a relationship between two things

Predicate the part of a sentence that tells something about the subject; it always contains a verb

Predicate adjective an adjective that follows a linking verb and describes the subject

Predicate noun a noun or pronoun that follows a linking verb and renames the subject

Preposition a word that links a noun or pronoun and other words in a sentence

Prepositional phrase a group of words that begins with a preposition and ends with a noun or pronoun

Pronoun a word that replaces a noun

Proper adjective the adjective form of a proper noun

Proper noun the name of a specific person, place, thing, or idea

Regular verb a verb whose past tense and past participle are formed by adding -d or -ed

Relative pronoun a pronoun that shows a relationship with a noun

Quotation marks the marks (" ") placed at the beginning and end of the words a person said

Second-person pronoun a pronoun that refers to the person who is being spoken to

Sentence a group of words that expresses a complete thought

Sentence fragment a group of words that does not express a complete thought

Series three or more similar words or groups of words

Simple tenses the present, past, and future forms of verbs

Singular noun the name of one person, place, thing, or idea

State-of-being verb a verb that tells something about the condition of the subject of a sentence; also called a linking verb

Subject the part of a sentence that tells who or what the sentence is about

Subject complement a noun, pronoun, or adjective that comes after a linking verb and adds meaning to the subject of a sentence

Subordinating conjunction a conjunction that connects a dependent clause to an independent clause

Superlative adjective an adjective that compares one noun with two or more

Superlative form the form of an adverb that compares more than two people or things

Tense the time when an action takes place

Third-person pronoun a pronoun that refers to the person or thing that is being talked about

Verb a word that shows action or a state of being

Verb phrase a main verb plus a helping verb

Verbal a verb form used as a noun or adjective in a sentence

Verbal phrase a verbal plus any words that help complete its meaning

Vowel these letters of the alphabet: *a, e, i, o, u,* and sometimes *y*